Ethernet LAN Cables:
For Computer Networks Professionals

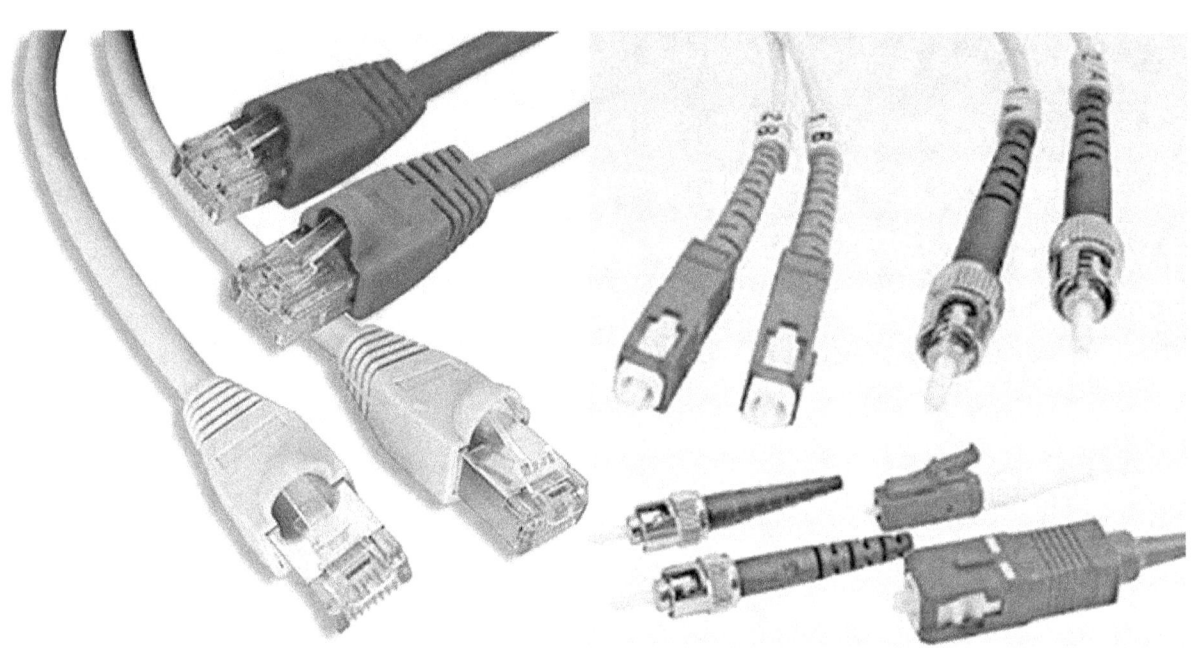

Ethernet LAN Cables:
For Computer Networks Professionals
Hakim Adiche

Hakim Adiche
2015

Copyright © 2015 by Hakim Adiche

All rights reserved. This book or any portion thereof may not be reproduced or used in any manner whatsoever without the express written permission of the publisher except for the use of brief quotations in a book review or scholarly journal.

First Printing: 2015

ISBN 978-1-329-18803-7

Dedication

To my lovely wife and children.

Thank you. Without your support and patience, I would have never achieved my dream.

Contents

About the Author xi
Preface xiii
Ethernet LAN Twisted Pair Cables 1
    Channel versus Permanent Link 2
    Stranded versus Solid Cables 2
        Bend Radius 3
    Electromagnetic Interference and Crosstalk Phenomena 4
        EMI 4
        Crosstalk 6
        Ethernet LAN Cable Twist Rate 7
    Unshielded Twisted Pair Cable - UTP 7
        Why Choose UTP Cables? 8
    Shielded Twisted Pair Cable - STP 8
        U/FTP 9
        F/UTP 10
        F/FTP 10
        S/FTP 11
        SF/UTP 12
    LAN Cable Categories 12
    Standardization Bodies – TIA/EIA and ISO/IEC 13
        TIA/EIA Category 3 Cable (ISO/IEC Class C) 14
        TIA/EIA Category 4 Cable (ISO/IEC Class D) 15
        TIA/EIA Category 5 Cable (ISO/IEC Class D) 15
        TIA/EIA Category 5_E Cable (ISO/IEC Class D_E) 15
        TIA/EIA Category 6 Cable (ISO/IEC Class E) 15
        TIA/EIA Category 6_A Cable (ISO/IEC Class E_A) 16
        Class F in ISO/IEC Standard 17
        Class F_A in ISO/IEC Standard 18
        Category 8 18
        Summary of Cable Types per Category 18
        Cross Reference ISO/IEC and TIA Naming Conventions 19
        TIA AND ISO STANDARDS REFERENCES 19
    LAN Cable Connectors 20
        Boot versus Bootless RJ-45 Connectors 22
        Stranded versus Solid RJ-45 Connectors 22
        Standard and Shielded RJ-45 Connectors 24
        Shielded Connectors per Cable Categories 24
        Other Types of 8P8C Connectors 26
        Augmented Registered Jack - ARJ45 27
        Cabling Specifications Terminologies 27
    LAN Cabling and Standards 27
        Straight-Through versus Crossover 28
        Terminating a Category $5/5_E/6$ UTP Cable 31

    Terminating a Category 6A F/UTP Cable 35
Wire Map Test 39
    Attenuation 41
    Insertion Loss 42
    Impedance Discontinuity 43
    Return Loss 43
    Connector Return Loss... 44
    Propagation Delay 44
    Time Domain Reflectometry 45
    Delay Skew 45
Twisted Pair Cable Crosstalk 46
    Near-End Cross-Talk - NEXT 46
    Far-End Cross-Talk – FEXT 47
    Power-Sum NEXT – PSNEXT 48
    Attenuation to Crosstalk Ratio - ACR 48
    Power Sum Attenuation to Cross-Talk Ratio – PSACR 49
    Attenuation to Crosstalk Ratio, Far-End (ACRF) (previously known as Equal-Level FEXT loss) 50
    Power Sum Attenuation to Crosstalk Ratio, Far-End (previously known as Power Sum ELFEXT loss) 51
Alien Cross-Talk 52
    Power Sum ANEXT 54
    Power Sum Alien Attenuation to Crosstalk Ratio Far – PS-AACRF (previously known as Power Sum Equal-Level FEXT or PS-AELFEXT) 54
Performance Comparison Chart 55
Flat Ethernet Cable 55
Power over Ethernet – PoE 57
Cable Fire Rating 58
    Plenum Grade 58
    Riser cable 59
    LSZH (Low Smoke Zero Halogen) 59
Summary about Copper Cables 59
    Advantages of Copper 60
    Disadvantages of Copper 60

Ethernet LAN Fiber Optic Cable 61
Optical Fiber Basics 61
Mode Field 62
Simplex versus Duplex Fiber Optic Cables 62
Single-Mode versus Multi-Mode Optical Fiber 63
    Single-Mode Operation 63
    Multimode Operation 64
Graded-Index and Step-Index Fiber 65
    Graded-Index Fiber 65
    Step-Index Fiber 66
Multimode Fibers Types 67
    OM1 67
    OM2 67

    OM3 67
    OM4 68
Fiber Optics Wavelengths **68**
Bend-Insensitive Multimode Fiber – BIMMF **69**
Higher Speed Fiber Links using MMFs **69**
Comparison of Light Sources **72**
Fiber Optic connectors **72**
    FC Connector 73
    ST Connector 73
    SC Connector 74
    MIC Connector 74
Modern Fiber Optic connectors **74**
    LC connector 74
Degrading Properties **75**
    Attenuation 75
    Dispersion 76
Latest Developments in Single Mode Optical Fibers **76**
Summary about Fiber Optic Cables **77**
    Advantages of Fiber over Copper Cables 77
    Disadvantages of Fiber Optic Cables 78

About the Author

Hakim Adiche is a computer networking instructor with more than 18 years of experience in the field of computer networks, networking protocols, and network programming. He is a lecturer in the King Fahd University of Petroleum and Minerals KFUPM, Saudi Arabia where he has written several laboratory experiments handouts for networking courses, taught different courses, short courses and training courses in topics related to computer networks. He has also conducted several workshops and technical presentations. He is a certified Cisco Academy instructor – CCAI and holds the CCNA, CCNP and CCIP certifications.

Hakim holds a master's degree in Computer Engineering and a B.S.E in Electrical Engineering.

Preface

Building a Local Area Network or LAN has always been an exciting enterprise for any computer networking professional. Usually, the initial effort is put on both hardware and software issues; from the hardware aspect, the network engineer or technician has to choose the right hardware platform including computers, network interface cards, switches, routers, wireless access points, etc.... On the other side and from the software aspect, the choice of Operating Systems such as Microsoft Windows, Linux, UNIX and OS X as well as networking based applications is a determinant factor in meeting the roles and objectives of any LAN.

All these efforts are necessary when building a LAN; however, cables used to connect between LAN devices are generally overlooked. In most of the time, Ethernet LAN cables are received ready made from manufacturers. The problems arise when a network engineer or technician wants to build a custom made cable that will run for a certain distance and support a specific speed while meeting the requirements and certifications in terms of the cabling standards.

I remember, long time ago when one of my students built a 15-meters long UTP cable on his own and tested it by connecting two PCs. He noticed that when large files were exchanged between these two PCs, the throughput barely reached 15% of the Fast Ethernet speed (that period was the beginning of the Fast Ethernet LAN technology era). He suspected that the problem was caused by either the Operating System, NIC drivers, or a virus causing some kind of bandwidth throttling. When I checked the cable, I noticed that the implementation did not follow the cabling standards, in many aspects. He then made a new UTP cable following the appropriate rules and standards. The result was a drastic improvement in bandwidth utilization during file transfers.

This simple example shows that a LAN can be implemented using the best hardware and software available. Networks professionals are well trained to make an excellent configuration of the hardware devices as well as software programs and tools. However, if the cabling is not made correctly, this will lead to very poor results and the LAN will run at less than its expected performance.

Nowadays, with the advent of high speed networks in server rooms and data centers, high performance cables with higher ratings are required. It is very important for every network engineer and technician to be aware about the challenges to be met when making and deploying customized cables. A minimum of knowledge is necessary to match the right cable with the right LAN performance.

The purpose of this book is to provide basic and vital information to the networks professionals who are mainly specialized in networking hardware and software configuration. It is a compilation of the most important cabling issues that need to be considered when deciding to build a new Ethernet LAN, the most important factors that will help make correct decisions on the type of cables that are needed for purchase, and the types of challenges expected with each type of cable.

Ethernet LAN Twisted Pair Cables

Ethernet Twisted Pair cables are the most widespread types of cables used in today's Ethernet LANs. A Twisted Pair cable consists of a bundle of eight copper wires, wrapped in an outer sheath or jacket, where each wire is protected by a colored insulation.
The insulation is used to avoid contacts that can cause short circuits between the copper wires, while the colors are meant for easy traceability of the wires at both ends of the cable, Figure 1.

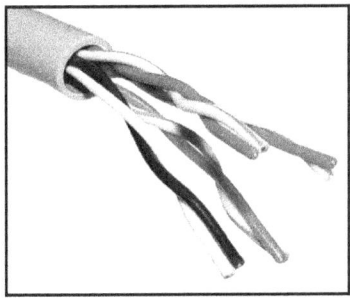

Figure 1: Twisted Pair Cable

Although silver has the best electrical conductivity compared to copper, however the later is the preferred conductor in Twisted Pair cables due to its lower cost. The eight colored wires are arranged in four pairs:

    Pair 1: Solid Blue   –   Blue with White stripes
    Pair 2: Solid Orange   –   Orange with White stripes
    Pair 3: Solid Green   –   Green with White stripes
    Pair 4: Solid Brown   –   Brown with White stripes

In some cables, the white striped wire insulation is completely white and does not show any other color. The jacket that surrounds and protects the wires inside a Twisted Pair Ethernet cable comes in all sorts of colors. In each pair, the wires are twisted to reduce inductive coupling or signal interference due to external noise that might degrade the signal. Some cables include a plastic *spline* to help keep the cable round and increase the distance between wire pairs to reduce crosstalk, Figure 2:

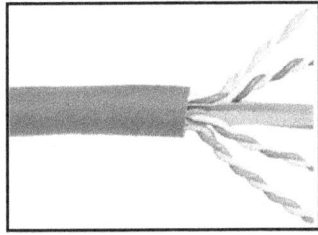

Figure 2: UTP Cable with Plastic *Spline*

Channel versus Permanent Link

Both Channel and Link terms are supported by the ISO/IEC standard. A permanent link is a connection from a Patch panel (usually on a rack) to a work area telecommunication outlet. It is also referred to as a horizontal cable since it lies horizontally on the floor. This is the most permanent fixture in structured cabling and cannot be easily taken apart. Once installed, it will be there and used for several years. The maximum permitted length of a permanent link is 90 meters, Figure 3.

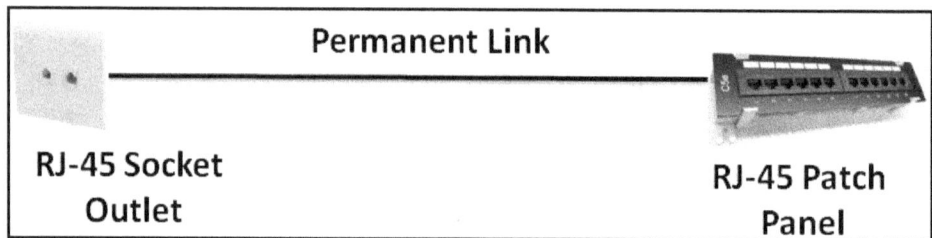

Figure 3: Permanent Link

A channel is a connection from an active device generally a switch located in a telecommunication cabinet to a network interface card of a computer. It includes the patch cords between a switch and a patch panel on a rack with a maximum length of 5 meters, the permanent link with a maximum length of 90 meters, and the work area cords between an end device and the work area outlet with a maximum length of 20 meters, as specified by ISO/IEC 11801 Ed. 2 standard. Under all circumstances, the maximum permitted length of a channel should not exceed 100 m, Figure 4.

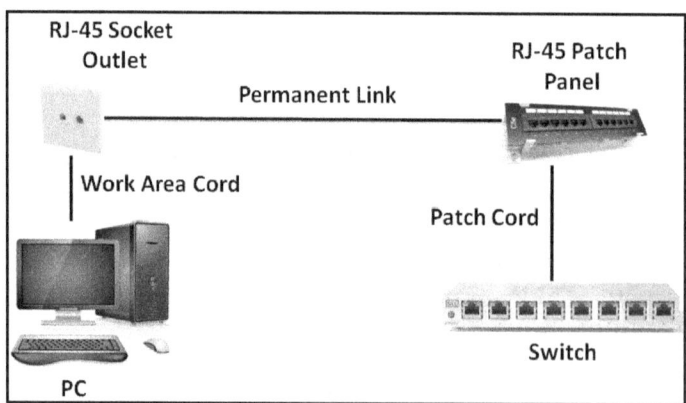

Figure 4: Channel Link

Note that all components in a channel must be of the same rating; otherwise the channel will perform at the lowest rating.

Stranded versus Solid Cables

In Stranded cables, the wires are made up of many fine metal filaments, which are twisted together to form a larger, thicker wire. This type of cables is more flexible than solid cables and is commonly used in home networking. The cable can be moved around the home without fear of cracking the copper wires inside.

Almost all patch cables that connect between switches and patch panels on racks are made with stranded wires. Stranded cables are cheaper compared to solid cables.

Solid cables have each of their conductors made of a solid copper wire. The whole cable is rigid with some resistance to bending. They are most often used in backbone cabling and permanent links (between a wall socket and a patch panel) where flexibility is not really needed, Figure 5.

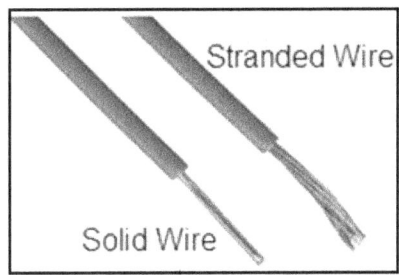

Figure 5: Solid Wire versus Stranded Wire

Theoretically, a solid cable supports a higher level of performance due to its superior electrical properties compared to stranded cables. The stranded conductor has a higher attenuation compared to solid conductor. This is the reason why, when used as a patch cord, its length should be kept 10 meters or less to reduce signal degradation.

When making a Twisted Pair cable using either solid or stranded wires, care should be taken to choose the appropriate hardware connector.

Connectors used with solid cables are different from those used with stranded cables. Although some vendors claim their connectors can work both ways, it is recommended to choose the right connector based on the wire inside the cable.

Note that, in general, stranded cables are cheaper compared to solid cables.

Bend Radius

Bend radius is the minimum radius a cable can be bent without damaging it, shortening its life or affecting its performance. The minimum bend radius for Category 5, 5e, and 6 cables is four times the cable diameter, which is approximately 1 inch. When cabling is bent beyond this specified minimum bend radius, it can cause transmission failures, Figure 6.

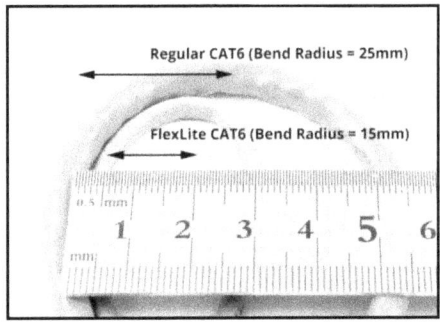

Figure 6: Examples of Bend Radii in Twisted Pair Cables

All pathways must maintain the minimum bend radius wherever the cable makes a bend. The installation of Twisted Pair cables should meet the TIA/EIA-568-A or ISO/IEC 11801 bend-radius requirements. If these requirements are not met, it will affect the twists rate and will reduce noise rejection.

Electromagnetic Interference and Crosstalk Phenomena

Data transmitted on a LAN cable, is subject to both Electromagnetic Interference - EMI and Crosstalk phenomena. The result is that many data frames in a LAN get corrupted or lost. This will cause a large number of retransmits that will slow down the whole data transfer process.

Consider a Fast Ethernet LAN with a maximum theoretical speed of 100 Mbps. If a LAN cable is subject to external noise or is not implemented correctly, the applications transferring data through that cable will suffer slow and poor performance.

Initially, one might suspect issues related to software such as bad Network Interface Card drivers coding, malwares, bugs in the applications, etc.... while in fact, the real problem can simply be a bad cable making that does not protect the wires carrying data from both EMI and crosstalk effects.

In this section, we are going to describe briefly how both EMI and Crosstalk signals can negatively impact data transmission performance on a LAN.

EMI

The wires in a LAN cable are subject to external noise such as EMI. A good making of a LAN cable eliminates or at least reduces its effect.

Going to the basics about data transmission, most applications require two wires. One wire transfers the actual data signal and the other wire connects to the ground or reference voltage. The difference of potential between the two wires will be the actual data signal that is fed to the receiving system, Figure 7.

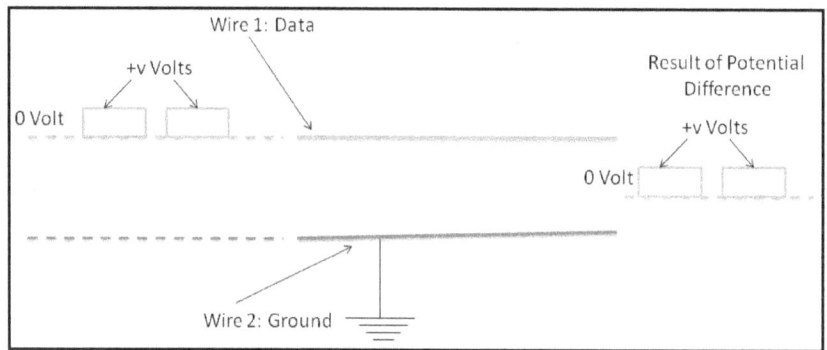

Figure 7: Data Transmission Using Two Wires

When an Electromagnetic wave affects a pair of wires running in parallel, it induces a transient electrical current in the first or closest wire and another transient electrical current in the second or furthest wire. These induced transit currents will affect and may corrupt transmitted data and make it unreadable at the receiver side, as depicted in Figure 8.

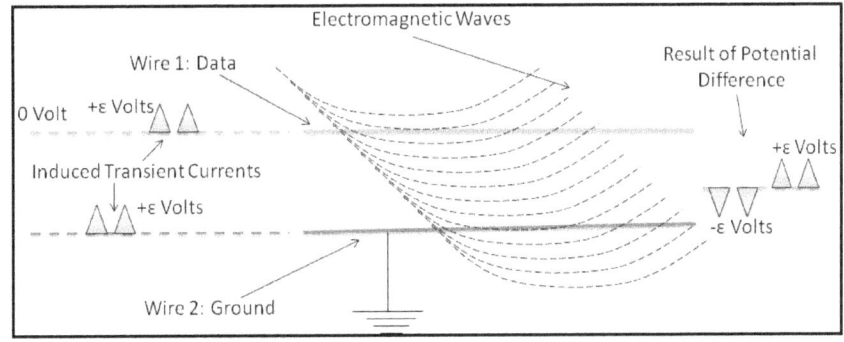

Figure 8: EMI Affecting Both Wires

The effect of EMI can be minimized by twisting the two wires (data and ground) at equal length. The Electromagnetic wave induces transient electrical current equally on both wires at the same time (common-mode signal effect). The transient electrical currents are then canceled when the difference signal is taken at the receiving end. The data signal is not altered and will be read correctly by the receiver, Figure 9.

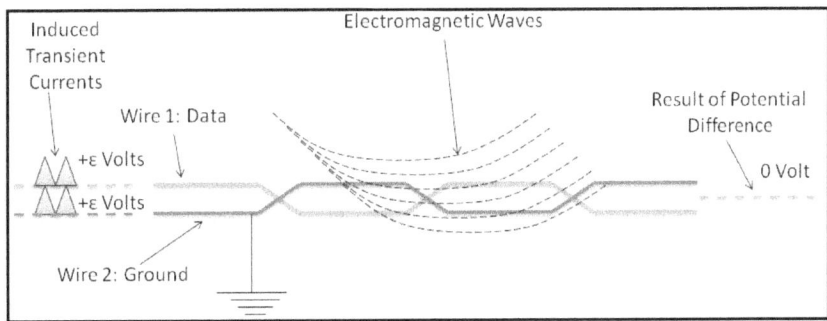

Figure 9: Cancelled EMI Effects

Another way to minimize the EMI effect is to surround the pairs of twisted wires with a metal shielding; a foil shield or a braided shield connected to the ground in order to dissipate the induced transient currents on the shield itself, Figure 10.

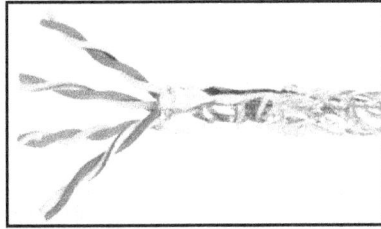

Figure 10: Shielded Twisted Pair Cable

Crosstalk

When a twisted pair cable runs in parallel with another conductor, during the transmission of data signals, a capacitor is formed between the two. The insulating material, in between, acts as a dielectric. Any data signal flowing in the twisted pair cable leaks to the conductor running in parallel and generates a crosstalk noise, Figure 11.

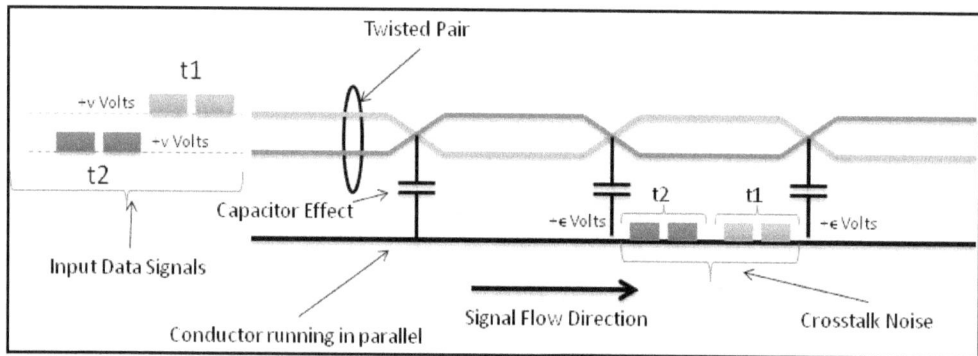

Figure 11: Crosstalk Effect

At time $t1$, a data signal with $+v$ Volts is fed to the first wire in the wire pair and gets leaked due to the capacitance effect into the conductor running in parallel. The leaked signal with $+\varepsilon$ Volts is the result of the crossing of the original signal being transmitted on the first wire. At time $t2$, another data signal with $+v$ Volts is fed to the second wire in the wire pair and gets leaked into the same conductor running in parallel. The leaked signal with $+\varepsilon$ Volts is also the result of the crossing of the original signal being transmitted on the second wire. Both leaked signals constitute crosstalk noise that will affect any data signal being transmitted on that same conductor wire running in parallel with the twisted pair. The main issue is the magnitude of the crosstalk noise. If the magnitude is high, then it will distort completely the original signal being transmitted on that wire. The receiver will not read or interpret the received signal correctly. Differential signaling prevents or reduces crosstalk problems. The data signal is converted into two complementary signals, by a differential driver. While one data signal on the first wire is positive ($+v$ Volts), the other data signal on the second wire of the twisted pair is negative by the same magnitude ($-v$ Volts), Figure 12.

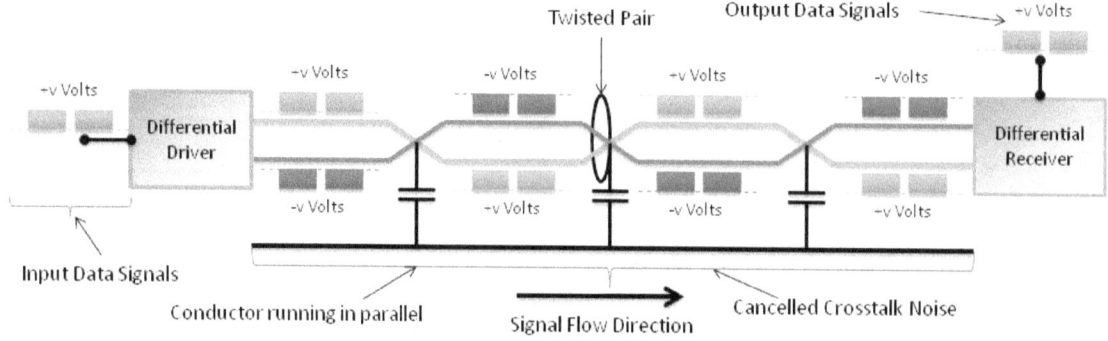

Figure 12: Differential Signaling

Both complementary data signals are sent simultaneously on the two wires of the same twisted pair. Their leaked signals on the conductor running in parallel will simply cancel each other due to their opposite polarity. The result is the elimination (in an ideal situation) or a reduction of the Crosstalk noise. At the end, the Differential Receiver recovers back the original data signal with the original polarity from the two complementary signals.

Ethernet LAN Cable Twist Rate

If adjacent wire pairs have the same twist rate and the source of EMI is uniform throughout the length of the twisted pair, the same wires of each pair could be repeatedly lying next to each other for the entire run, partially and negatively affecting the differential signaling to eliminate or reduce crosstalk noise. For this reason it is commonly specified that, at least for cables containing small numbers of pairs, the twist rates must differ. At each half twist, the wire nearest to the source of EMI is swapped in order to keep the induced transient electrical current common-mode and to cancel or reduce crosstalk noise. The twist rate is not specified in the standard. However, observed measurements on one sample of Category 5 cable provided the following results, Table 1:

Pair color	cm per turn	Turns per meter
Green	1.53	65.2
Blue	1.54	64.8
Orange	1.78	56.2
Brown	1.94	51.7

Table 1: Twisted Rates

Unshielded Twisted Pair Cable - UTP

This is the most widely used cable in modern Ethernet LANs, Figure 13. Although this cable is cheap and easy to implement, it is however subject to external noise and signal interference.

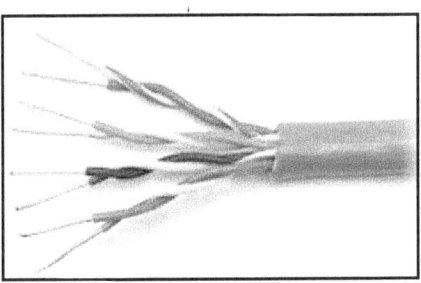

Figure 13: Unshielded Twisted Pair Cable

Care should be taken when this cable runs in an area with EMI and electrical noise that may affect, distort, and corrupt the electrical signals in the wires. The result will be an increase of the frame loss ratio and poor LAN performance.

Why Choose UTP Cables?

The most interesting reasons behind the choice of a UTP cable are listed below:

1. UTP cables are used to support different types of communications such as data, voice and video.
2. UTP cables are Color-coded and allow the tracing of wires between the ends of the cables even if the cables have long runs.
3. UTP cables with their transceivers and connectors are less expensive than fiber optic cables.
4. UTP cables are very easy to build, install, terminate and troubleshoot.

Shielded Twisted Pair Cable - STP

STP traditionally refers to the older Type1 Token Ring cabling, however, the new shielded twisted pair cables are different from the STP but they are still referred to using this acronym.

Twisted pair cables are often shielded in an attempt to prevent EMI. Most applications for the STP cable are between equipment racks and buildings.

Because the shielding is made of metal, it may also serve as a ground. Usually a shielded twisted pair cable has a special grounding wire added called a drain wire which is electrically connected to the shield, Figure 14.

Figure 14: Shielded Twisted Pair Cable with Drain Wire

The drain wire simplifies connection to the ground at the connectors, Figure 15.

Figure 15: Drain Wire Fixed on the Connector

Shielded cables have some special grounding concerns because one, and only one, end of a shielded cable should be connected to an earth ground; issues arise when people inadvertently cause grounding loops to occur by connecting the shield at both ends of a cable to the ground or cause the shield to act as an antenna because it is not grounded.

The shielding can be applied to individual pairs of wires, or to the collection of pairs. When shielding is applied to the collection of pairs, this is referred to as screening.

Shielding provides an electric conductive barrier to attenuate EMI and provides conduction path by which induced currents can be circulated and leaked to the ground via ground reference connection.

There are two types of shielding used in twisted pair cables; the braided shield and the foiled shield; the braided shield provides good protection from low frequency interferences, whereas the foil shield provides better protection over a wider range of frequencies.

Both foil and braid shields are sometimes used in combination for the best protection of the data signal flowing through the cable wires in a noisy environment.

There are different shielding configurations for shielded twisted pair cables, as described below using ISO/IEC 11801 standard names:

U/FTP

The Unshielded Foiled Twisted Pair cable offers foil shield for each individual twisted pair of wires, Figure 16.

Figure 16: U/FTP Cable

The U/FTP shielding protects from EMI entering or exiting the twisted pairs as well as from crosstalk, Figure 17.

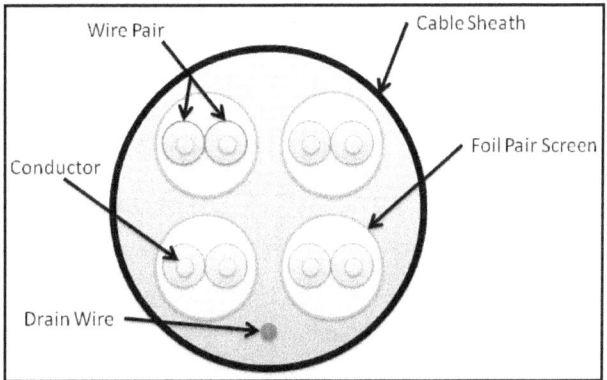

Figure 17: Cross Section of U/FTP Cable

F/UTP

The Foil over Unshielded Twisted Pair cable offers an overall sheath shield across all of the pairs inside the cable, Figure 18.

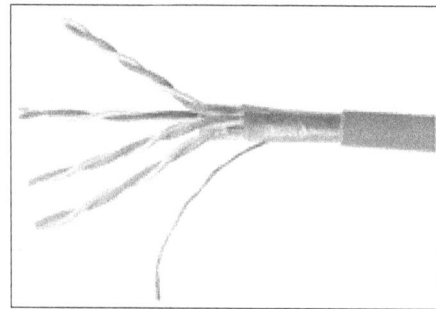

Figure 18: F/UTP Cable with a grounding wire

The F/UTP uses a foil shield screen wrapped around all cable pairs. This type of shielding protects from EMI entering or exiting the cable, Figure 19.

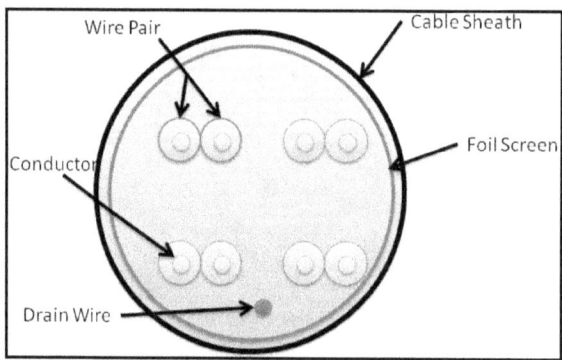

Figure 19: Cross Section of F/UTP Cable

F/FTP

The Screened over Foiled Shielded Twisted Pair cable offers an overall sheath shield across all of the pairs and individually foiled twisted wire pairs, Figure 20.

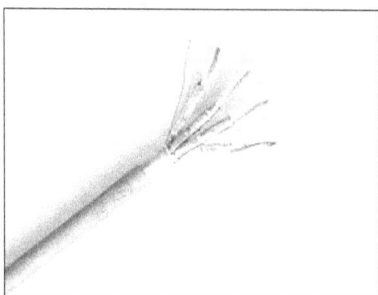

Figure 20: F/FTP Cable

The F/FTP uses a foil shield screen wrapped around all cable pairs and a foil shield for each twisted wire pair to protect against EMI entering or exiting the cable and the wire pairs as well as crosstalk between the wire pairs, Figure 21.

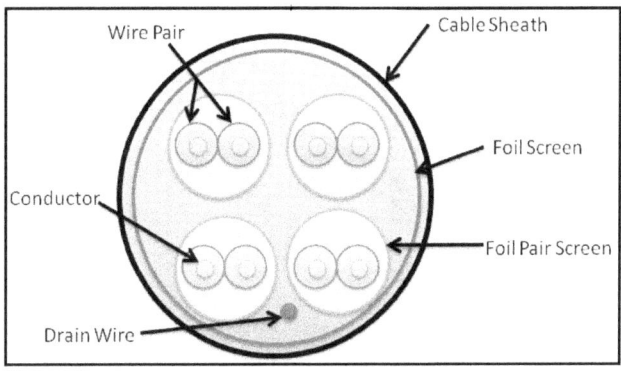

Figure 21: Cross Section of F/FTP Cable

S/FTP

The braided with foiled twisted pair cable uses a braid shield screen wrapped around all cable twisted pairs and individually foiled cable twisted pairs, Figure 22.

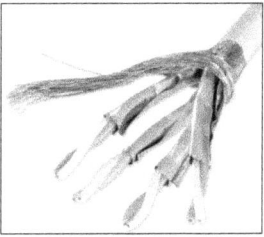

Figure 22: Screened Shielded Twisted Pair

This type of cabling protects cable from external EMI entering or exiting the cable and wire pairs, and also eliminates or reduces crosstalk between wire pairs, Figure 23.

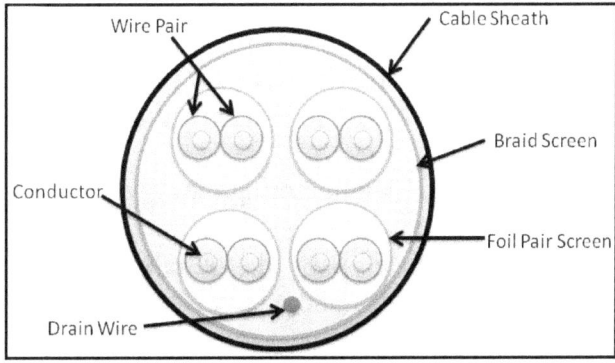

Figure 23: Cross section of S/FTP Cable

SF/UTP

The braided and foil over unshielded Twisted Pair cable is a kind of cable which has braided shield and foiled shield together wrapped around all the cable twisted wire pairs, Figure 24.

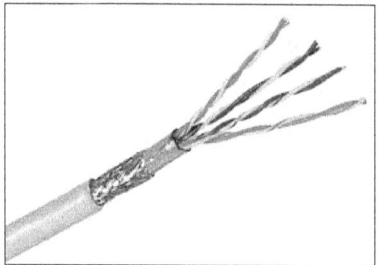

Figure 24: SF/UTP Cable

Usually, it is used for outdoor cables for better protection against electrical signals and physical effects, Figure 25.

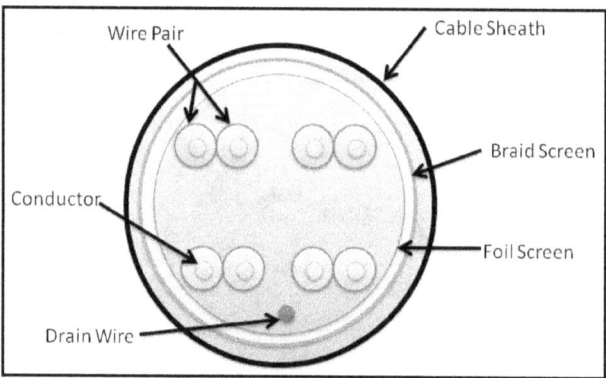

Figure 25: SF/UTP Cable

LAN Cable Categories

Twisted pair cables are rated based on their categories. All cable categories differ in the following:

1. Amount of bandwidths and frequencies they can support.
2. Distance for which they support such bandwidth while keeping the original signal in good shape.
3. Amount of copper used in manufacturing the wires.
4. Number of twists per wire pair.
5. Ability to eliminate or reduce EMI and crosstalk interferences.
6. Size or diameter of copper wire and which is measured using the American Wire Gauge (AWG) unit.

Note that since 1995, the UTP cables with solid conductors for backbone cabling are required to be no thicker than 22 AWG and no thinner than 24 AWG, or 26 AWG for shorter-distance cabling. This standard has been retained with the 2009 revision of ANSI TIA/EIA 568.

On most LAN cables, a label printed on the jacket indicates the category of the cable, Figure 26.

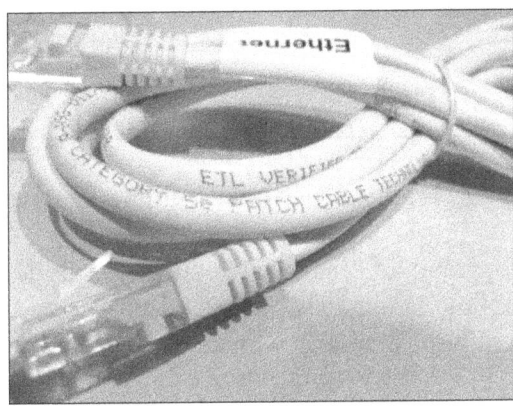

Figure 26: Category Label

Standardization Bodies – TIA/EIA and ISO/IEC

The TIA/EIA (Telecommunications Industries Association/ Electronic Industries Association) and ISO/IEC (International Standard Organization/International Electronic Components) committees are the leaders in the development of structured cabling standards with the purpose to ensure the best performance for signal transmission in newer cables. It is worth mentioning that the term *link* refers to *cable*:

1. TIA/EIA standard 568 is a US standard that defines categories of unshielded twisted pair cable systems, with different levels of performance. It is also responsible for UTP pin/pair assignments for eight-conductor 100-ohm balanced twisted pair cabling. These assignments are named T568A and T568B. The cabling components included in this standard are cables, connecting hardware and patch cords. These cabling components are characterized by a performance Category and are connected together to form a permanent link or channel that are also described by a performance Category. To give a simple example, a channel link connecting a PC to an Ethernet switch should have the same rating for the permanent link, the patch cord and the connectors. All these elements should be of the same Category to ensure maximum performance. If Category 6 cable is used, then the connectors and patch cords should mate the same rating as this category, Figure 27

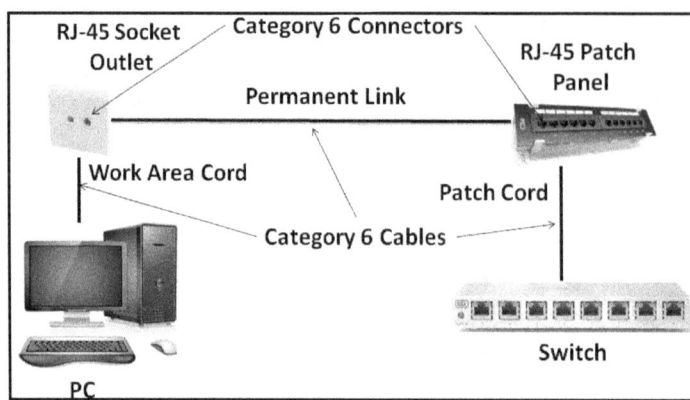

Figure 27: TIA/EIA Category Cabling Components

2. ISO/IEC 11801 is an international standard that defines several link/channel *Classes* and cabling *Categories* of twisted-pair copper interconnects, which differ in the maximum frequency for which a certain channel performance is required.

The connecting hardware components are characterized by a performance Category while permanent links and channels are described by a performance Class. If Class E cable is used in the entire channel (work area cord, permanent link and patch cord), then the cable connectors should match Category 6, Figure 28.

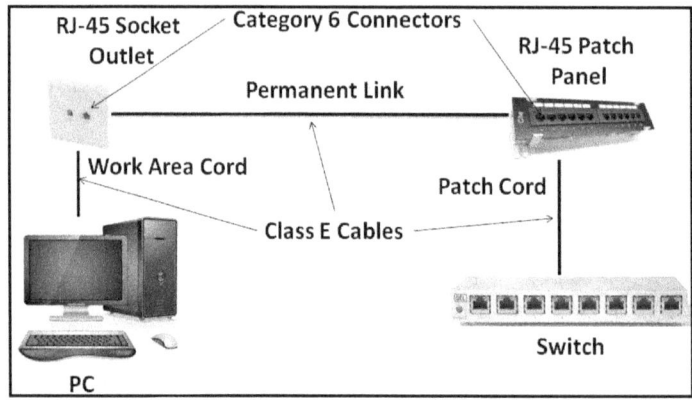

Figure 28: ISO/IEC Class/Category Cabling Components

TIA/EIA Category 3 Cable (ISO/IEC Class C)

Category 3 cables were used in the early 90's for wiring offices and homes. They are still used in two-line phone configurations, but not anymore in wired networking. This cable category supports the Ethernet standard 10BASE-T to achieve a speed of 10 Mbps over a maximum distance of 100 meters. It is rated for a maximum frequency of 16 MHz. All eight wires are 24 AWG and only two pairs are used to transmit and receive data. The other two pairs are not used except in some applications where they are integrated in the telephone network.

While theoretically limited to 10BASE-T Ethernet, Category 3 cables can support 100BASE-T4 Ethernet protocol by using all four pairs of wires instead of two pairs only to achieve 100 Mbps speed. However, 100 Mbps on Category 3 UTP cable did not get much attention and popularity because of its lack of backward compatibility with the 10BASE-T standard which used only two wire pairs for data communication.

TIA/EIA Category 4 Cable (ISO/IEC Class D)

Category 4 cable specification supports a data rate of 16 Mbps with a maximum rated frequency of 20 MHz. For a brief period, it was used for 10BASE-T, and 100BASE-T4 networks, but was quickly replaced by Category 5 cable which appeared during the same period and with better performance. The Category 4 cable specification is not recognized by the TIA/EIA-568 data cabling standards.

TIA/EIA Category 5 Cable (ISO/IEC Class D)

Category 5 cable specification was ratified in 1991 to support the 100BASE-T Ethernet standard with backward compatibility with the 10BASE-T Ethernet standard.
This cable category uses two of the four 24-AWG wire pairs to send and receive at 100 Mbps over a maximum distance of 100 meters, exactly as the 10BASE-T standard. It is rated for a maximum frequency of 100 MHz.

TIA/EIA Category 5_E Cable (ISO/IEC Class D_E)

Category 5_E specification was ratified in 1999 and requirements were first published in 2000. The cables are rated at the same maximum frequency (100 MHz) as Category 5 cables and some manufacturers raise the maximum frequency to 250 MHz. This cable category uses four-connector channel with support of the Ethernet standard 1GBASE-T. It is backward compatible with 100BASE-T and 10BASE-T Ethernet standards. The 24 AWG wire pairs are twisted more tightly to eliminate or reduce crosstalk. Some manufacturers propose shielded cables (F/UTP) with 26 AWG stranded wires. Nowadays, a Category 5_E cable is considered legacy and should not be deployed in new cabling installations.

TIA/EIA Category 6 Cable (ISO/IEC Class E)

The Category 6 specification was published in 2002 by TIA/EIA (the same time as ISO Class F/Category 7). This Category of UTP cables supports the Ethernet standard 1GBASE-T and is backward compatible with the 10BASE-T and 100BASE-T Ethernet standards. Category 6 cables can also support the 10GBASE-T Ethernet standard over a limited distance of 55 meters in a favorable environment and 37 meters in a hostile and noisy environment. They are rated for a maximum frequency 250 MHz and some manufacturers provide rating for up to 400 MHz.
The solid wire diameter ranges between 22 and 24 AWG, while shielded cables (F/UTP) with stranded wires proposed by some manufacturers have diameters of 26 AWG. A category 6 cable may include a longitudinal plastic separator, or *spline*, to isolate the four twisted wire pairs and increase distance between them to reduce crosstalk, Figure 29.

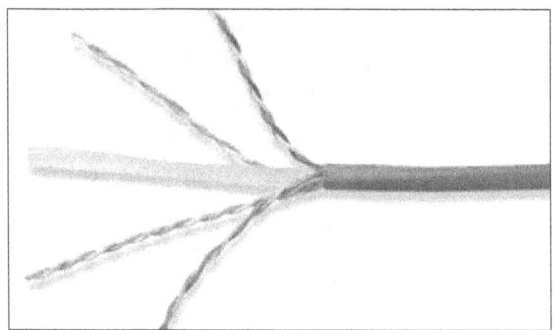

Figure 29: Category 6 LAN Cable with a *spline*

Category 6 cables are considered as the standard choice for projects, nowadays and should be used to upgrade old cables and to build new LAN with support of the 1Gbase Ethernet standard; the 10-Gigabit Ethernet active hardware is currently very expensive to be deployed in a LAN. However, when it comes to network backbones and data centers following the TIA/EIA cabling standard where 10GBASE-T Ethernet standard is much interesting for moving data, Category 6_A cables should be considered.

TIA/EIA Category 6_A Cable (ISO/IEC Class E_A)

Category 6_A specification was published in February 2008. Category 6_A cables support the Ethernet standard 10GBASE-T and are backward compatible with the other 10BASE-T, 100BASE-T, and 1GBASE-T Ethernet standards over a maximum distance of 100 meters.

Category 6_A standard is rated for a maximum frequency of 500 MHz; however, some manufacturers provide support for 550 MHz. It comes in unshielded (UTP) as well as shielded version (F/UTP).

The solid wire diameter ranges from 22 to 24 AWG, while shielded cables version (F/UTP) with stranded wires proposed by some manufacturers have diameters of 26 AWG.

The Category 6_A solid wire cables are larger in diameter than Category 6 and category 5e and are less susceptible to EMI and crosstalk compared to the previous cable categories.

The Outside Diameter (O.D) of a Category 6_A UTP cable diameter (0.354 inch) is larger than that of the Category 6_A F/UTP cable (0.265). More F/UTP cables can fit in a cable conduit compared to the UTP cables. It is claimed that Category 6_A F/UTP provides a minimum of 35% more fill capacity than Category 6_A UTP cable.

Additionally, not only security is enhanced with the shielded category 6_A cable, but the cable is also lighter and supports high port density. All these mentioned factors contribute in reducing the installation cost using F/UTP cables instead of UTP.

Shielded category 6_A F/UTP cables are easier to implement with less problems and restrictions to provide support for the 10GBASE-T Ethernet standard compared to Category 6 cables with an upward bend radius of 30 mm.

Some cable installers claimed that Category 6_A cables installation cost about 33% more than the same with Category 5_E cables.

The lifespan of a Category 6_A cable is from 15 to 20 years and during which period equipment can be replaced three to four times. However, Category 6_A cables suffer from limitations such as:

1. Larger diameter compared to previous cable categories because of shielding and the UTP spacing inside the cable.
2. Higher operating frequencies creating alien crosstalk problems.
3. Shielded Category 6_A cables require grounding and bounding.

Category 6_A cables have seen improvements through several generations, Table 2:

Generation	Outside Diameter O.D
Gen 1	9.07 mm
Gen 2	8.90 mm
Gen 3	8.20 mm
Gen 4	7.30 mm

Table 2: Category 6A Cables Generations

Some vendors claim that the new 4th Category 6_A solution offers up to 2-3% project cost savings compared to the existing Category 6 UTP solutions.
Other manufacturers have developed restricted Category 6_A systems with smaller cable and patch cords to support 10GBASE-T Ethernet standard for lengths less than the full standard.
Recently in spring 2015, a *Mini-6_A* cable has been introduced. With a solid wire diameter of 28 AWG, it is 23 percent smaller than existing Category 6_A offerings, has a 38 percent smaller cross sectional area and is 33 percent lighter than standard UTP patch cables. This was achieved by eliminating the *spline* which normally separates cable pairs in high specification Category 6 cables. However, a *Mini-6_A* cable has distance limitation with a maximum reach of 56 meters.

Class F in ISO/IEC Standard

Class F/Category 7 (ISO/IEC), published in 2002, is a fully shielded system; overall shield with individual shielded pairs; S/FTP.
It was defined under the ISO/IEC 11801 standard and has a 15-year lifecycle.
A Class F cable should use a Category 7 connector with the same rating to achieve the same expected performance. The cost of a Class 7 cabling solution is less than that of a Fiber Optic counterpart.
TIA does not recognize Class F cable specifications. TIA never developed specifications for what should have been called Category 7 cable.
Class F supports the Ethernet standard 10GBASE-T and is backward compatible with 10BASE-T, 100BASE-T and 1GBASE-T Ethernet standards over a maximum distance of 100 meters.
Class F cables are rated for a maximum frequency of 600 MHz and offer better performance compared to Category 6_A or Class E_A cables.
However, Class F can be backward compatible with Class D (using Category 5e elements and connectors) and Class E (using Category 6 elements and connectors). The solid wire diameter ranges from 22 to 24 AWG.
In order to achieve the maximum performance at 600 MHz, a Class F cabling system should use non-RJ style plug and socket interfaces such as GG45 and TERA.

Class F_A in ISO/IEC Standard

Class F_A/Category7_A specification was published in February 2008. Class F_A cable is a fully shielded system (S/FTP) and supports the 10GBASE-T IEEE Ethernet standard and is backward compatible with 10BASE-T, 100BASE-T and 1GBASE-T Ethernet standards over a maximum distance of 100 meters.

Class F_A category is rated for a maximum frequency of 1000 MHz using the S/FTP shielding solution.

It also supports 40GBASE-T Ethernet standard up to 50 meters and 100 GBASE-T with a maximum reach of 15 meters.

The solid wire diameter ranges from 22 to 24 AWG.

As in Class F, to achieve the maximum performance at 1000 MHz, non-RJ style plug and socket interfaces such as GG45 and TERA should be used to terminate the Class F_A cables.

Category 8

Since TIA/EIA did not develop Category 7 or 7_A specifications and to avoid confusion with Class F and Class F_A from ISO/IEC, they decided that their next higher cable specification will be named Category 8.

The Category 8 cable is intended to provide support for 40 Gbps speed over copper-based Ethernet applications as defined by the Next Generation Cabling standard (IEEE TR42.7) established in 2011.

The total channel length to be allowed for Category 8 cable is expected to be 50 meters.

The TIA/EIA is planning for Category 8 cable with a frequency rating of up to 2 GHz based on an extended performance of Category 6A cable. Remember again, TIA/EIA did not develop any specifications for Categories 7 and 7_A cables.

In Europe, the ISO/IEC is looking at two options:

1. Class I/Category 8.1 (cable/connector) supports a minimum cable design based on U/FTP or F/UTP. It is fully backward compatible and interoperable with Class E_A using 8P8C connectors.
2. Class II/Category 8.2 (cable/connector) supports a minimum cable design based on F/FTP or S/FTP. It is interoperable with Class F_A using 8P8C connectors; TERA, GG45, and ARJ45 connectors.
3. It should be noted that Class II has higher NEXT and FEXT performance because each of the four pairs are individually shielded.

All of these options are considering shielded cables and connectors because of alien crosstalk problems.

As of January 2014, draft versions of ISO/IEC TR 11801-99-1 and ANSI/TIA-568-C.2-1 have been aligned to reduce the difference between TIA Categories 8 specification and both ISO Class I/Category 8.1 and Class II/Category 8.2 specifications.

Summary of Cable Types per Category

Table 3 summarized the main information with respect to each cable *Category* or *Class*:

Cable Category	Cable Type
Category 5E	UTP or FTP
Category 6	UTP, FTP or SFTP
Category 6A	UTP, FTP or SFTP
Category 7	SFTP
Category 7A	SFTP

Table 3: Cable Types per Category

Cross Reference ISO/IEC and TIA Naming Conventions

Table 4 depicts the naming conventions used between the two standards; TIA/EIA and ISO/IEC:

ISO (Cabling)	ISO (Components)	TIA (Cabling and Components)
Class D	Category 5E	Category 5E
Class E	Category 6	Category 6
Class E_A	Category 6_A	Category 6_A
Class F	Category 7	No Specification
Class F_A	Category 7_A	No Specification
Class I	Category 8.1	Category 8
Class II	Category 8.2	Class II

Table 4: TIA/EIA and ISO/IEC Naming Conventions

ISO/IEC Class I/Category 8.1 and TIA Category 8 will not be backward compatible with ISO/IEC Class F_A/Category 7_A; however it is backward compatible with ISO/IEC Class E_A/Category 6_A.

ISO/IEC Class II/Category 8.2 is backward compatible with ISO/IEC Class F_A/Category 7_A.

TIA AND ISO STANDARDS REFERENCES

The TIA and ISO standards references are represented in Table 5:

	TIA/EIA Standards
Category 5e	ANSI/TIA-568-C.2, Balanced Twisted-Pair Telecommunications Cabling and Components Standard, 2009
Category 6	ANSI/TIA-568-C.2, Balanced Twisted-Pair Telecommunications Cabling and Components Standard, 2009
Category 6A	ANSI/TIA-568-C.2, Balanced Twisted-Pair Telecommunications Cabling and Components Standard, 2009
	ISO/IEC Standards
Class D	ISO/IEC 11801, 2nd Ed., Information technology – Generic Cabling for Customer Premises, 2002
Class E	ISO/IEC 11801, 2nd Ed., Information technology – Generic Cabling for Customer Premises, 2002
Class EA	Amendment 1 to ISO/IEC 11801, 2nd Ed., Information technology – Generic Cabling for Customer Premises, 2008
Class F	ISO/IEC 11801, 2nd Ed., Information technology – Generic Cabling for Customer Premises, 2002
Class FA	Amendment 1 to ISO/IEC 11801, 2nd Ed., Information technology – Generic Cabling for Customer Premises, 2008

Table 5: TIA and ISO Standards References

LAN Cable Connectors

The 8P8C RJ-45 modular plug and jack was originally patented in 1975 by Western Electric Company under AT&T.

Ethernet LAN cables use 8P8C modular RJ-45 connectors standardized under IEC 60603-7 with different categories of performance.

The 8P8C RJ-45 connector has two paired components; the male plug; Figure 30 and the female jack; Figure 31.

Figure 30: RJ-45 Male Plug (Connector) (8P8C)

Figure 31: RJ-45 Female Jack (Socket) (8P8C)

The physical dimensions of the male and female connectors are specified in ANSI/TIA-1096-A and ISO-8877 standards and normally wired to the T568A and T568B pin-outs specified in the TIA/EIA-568 standard.

The plugs are used to build and terminate cables, Figure 32, while jacks are used for fixed locations such as mount-boxes, wall plates, panels, and on the equipment such as hubs and switches (although switches have now replaced hubs), Figure 33.

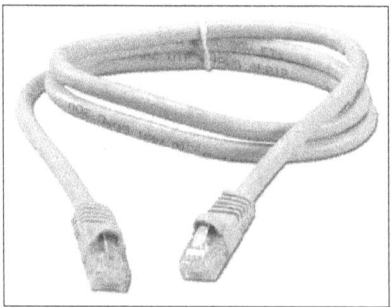

Figure 32: UTP Cable with RJ-45 Plugs

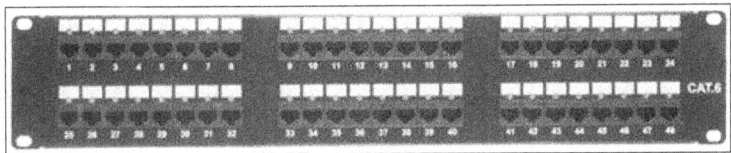

Figure 33: RJ-45 Patch Panel with RJ-45 Female Jacks

The 8P8C RJ-45 connectors shows two numbers; the 8 followed by *P* represents the number of positions, while the second 8, followed by *C*, represents the number of contacts.
In other words, the connector has eight pins and each pin makes a contact with one cable wire.
The contacts or pins positions are numbered sequentially starting from 1 to 8. When viewed head on with the lock release clip on the bottom, jacks will have pin number 1 on the left and plugs will have it on the right, Figure 34.

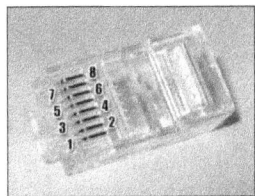

Figure 34: RJ-45 Pins Positions

RJ-45 connectors look similar to the RJ-11 four-wire connectors used in the telephone network but wider, Figure 35.

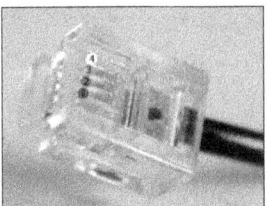

Figure 35: RJ-11 Connector

A physical comparison between RJ-45 and RJ-11 connectors is illustrated in Figure 36.

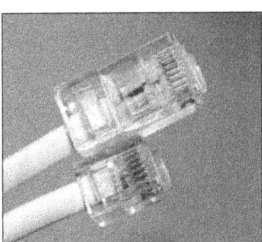

Figure 36: RJ-45 (top) and RJ-11 (bottom) connectors

The physical dimensions and high-frequency performance of RJ-45 connectors used for data communications are specified in the International Standard IEC 60603.

Boot versus Bootless RJ-45 Connectors

Some twisted pair cables are implemented with boots to keep them from snagging (anti-snag boots) and to protect clips from breaking when they are pulled, Figure 37.

Figure 37: RJ-45 Connectors with Snagless Boots

Bootless twisted pair cables are commonly implemented as well, Figure 38. Although these connectors might be subjected to snagging and have their clips broken when they are pulled, however, they are not to be played with or manipulated on a frequent basis.
The main advantage is the economy done on the price of the boots.

Figure 38: Bootless RJ-45 Connectors

Stranded versus Solid RJ-45 Connectors

The RJ45 connector has to be chosen based on whether the Twisted Pair cable to be implemented has solid or stranded wires.
When looking at the RJ-45 connector from the side, the tiny metal connector pins have prongs that contact the wire copper metal to make a conductive connection, Figure 39.

Figure 39: Wire Conductor Contact with Prongs

RJ-45 connector with stranded wire has a 2-prong style contacts to straddle the strands of each wire conductor, Figure 40.

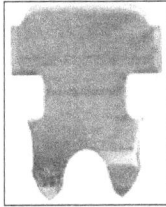

Figure 40: Stranded (2-Prong)

Another RJ-45 connector that supports stranded wires has jagged end style contacts to get embedded into the strands of each wire conductor, Figure 41.

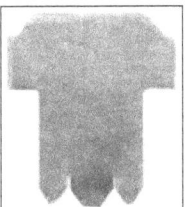

Figure 41: Stranded Only

RJ-45 connector with solid wires has longer 3-prong style contacts to wraps around the wire conductor instead of penetrating it, Figure 42.

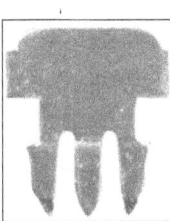

Figure 42: Solid (3-Prong)

Most RJ45 connectors use 2 prongs which penetrate the conductor itself. This is not desirable, since a solid wire conductor has the tendency to break when penetrated by the prong. Figure 43, below, shows a comparison between the stranded and solid RJ-45 connectors.

Figure 43: Solid (Left) and Stranded (Right) RJ-45 connectors

Standard and Shielded RJ-45 Connectors

The 8P8C RJ-45 connectors come in two types; Standard and Shielded:

Standard connectors are used whenever the UTP cables run in an area with no EMI problems that may affect and distort the data signals in the cable wires. An illustration of a standard RJ-45 connector is shown in Figure 44.

Figure 44: Standard RJ-45 Connector

Note that the wires should have the appropriate diameter to fit inside the pins of the RJ-45 connector.
Shielded connectors are used not only if the twisted pair cables run in a noisy environment but also in higher speed and higher performance situation. Shielded RJ-45 connectors come in two different designs, Figures 45 and 46:

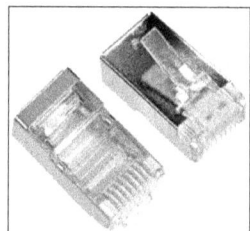

Figure 45: RJ-45 Connectors with Internal Ground

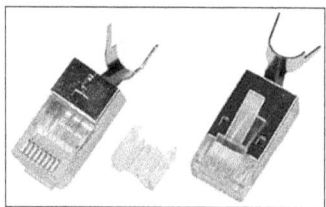

Figure 46: RJ-45 Connectors with External Ground

These two ground designs are suitable in carrying induced noise through the braided and foiled shields into the drain wire that connects directly to the internal or external ground of the RJ-45 connector.

Shielded Connectors per Cable Categories

Each cable Category has the appropriate shielded RJ-45 plug with the same rating to ensure the best performance.

Below are different illustrations of shielded RJ-45 connectors for different cables Categories:

1. Shielded Category 5 RJ-45 connector designed to support 24 AWG solid conductors:

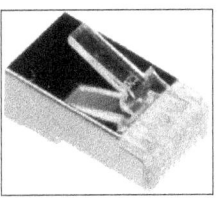

2. Shielded Category 5e RJ-45 connector designed to support 24-26 AWG wire conductors:

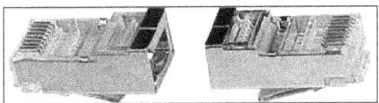

Solid Wires Connectors

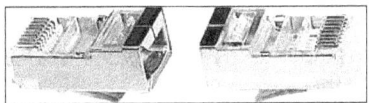

Stranded Wires Connectors

3. Shielded Category 6 RJ-45 connector designed to support 24-26 AWG wire conductors:

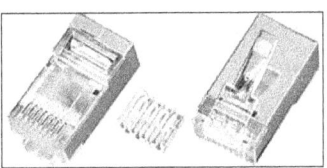

Stranded Wires Connectors

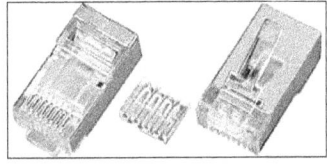

Solid Wires Connectors

4. Shielded Category 6_A RJ-45 connector designed to support 23-26 AWG Stranded Conductors

5. Shielded Category 7 RJ-45 connector designed to support 23-26 AWG Stranded Conductors

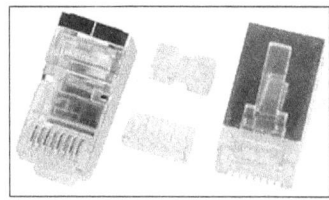

Starting from 2010, all manufacturers provided support to shielded RJ-45 connector for their Ethernet 10-Gbps products on Category 6A copper.

However, since the RJ-45 connector is limited to 10-Gbps speed, other types of connectors should be used for higher bandwidths.

Other Types of 8P8C Connectors

The ISO/IEC standards; Class F and Class F_A cables can be terminated with the 8P8C compatible GG45 (GG stands for Giga Gate, and 45 is to remind the backward compatibility with the RJ-45) shielded electrical connector which is used for high-speed LAN cabling with a frequency up to 600 MHz and 1000 MHz, or with TERA connector (launched in 1999) which is a shielded twisted pair connector with the characterized performance of up to 1000 MHz, Figure 47.

When combined with GG45 or TERA connectors, Class F cables can reach transmission frequencies of up to 600 MHz and up to 1000MHz for Class F_A.

These connectors are suitable in Data Centers where speeds of 40 Gbps or 100 Gbps are suitable, knowing that RJ-45 plugs have found limitation to 10 Gbps as their best performance.

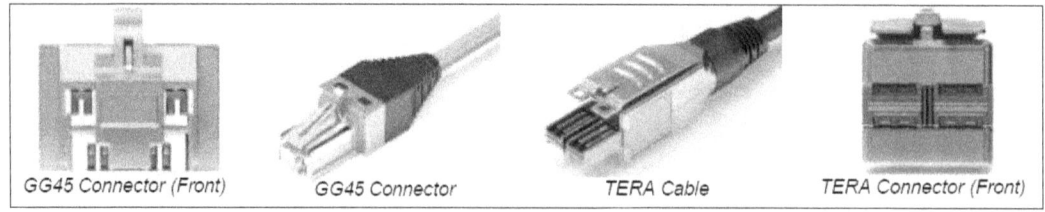

Figure 47: GG45 and TERA Connectors

The ISO recommends the GG45 as the preferred connector for Data Center installations because of its backward compatibility with RJ-45 connectors, but allows the TERA connector to be used where cable sharing is more important than backwards compatibility.

Augmented Registered Jack - ARJ45

The ARJ45 is a connector, Figure 48, for high speed applications such as Class F_A installations as defined by the standard ISO/IEC 11801 and 10, 40 and 100 GBASE-T Ethernet standards for transmission over copper cables.

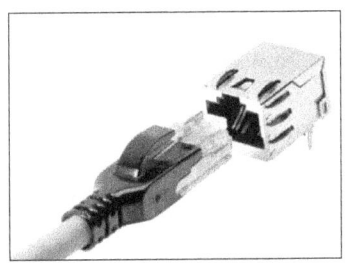

Figure 48: ARJ45 Connectors

ARJ45 complies with the international standard IEC 61076-3-110 and operates in the frequency spectrum between 600 MHz to 5 GHz with twisted shielded pair.
ARJ45 reduces crosstalk to 35 dB or better at 5GHz and reaches a performance at 1000 MHz that corresponds to Category 7_A connecting hardware.

Cabling Specifications Terminologies

The technical requirements of TIA and ISO are very similar for various grades of cabling, however the terminology defers, Table 6.

FREQUENCY BANDWIDTH	TIA (COMPONENTS)	TIA (CABLING)	ISO (COMPONENTS)	ISO (CABLING)
100 MHz	Category 5e	Category 5e	Category 5e	Class D
250 MHz	Category 6	Category 6	Category 6	Class E
500 MHz	Category 6A	Category 6A	Category 6A	Class EA
600 MHz	N/S	N/S	Category 7	Class F
1000 MHz	N/S	N/S	Category 7A	Class FA

Table 6: TIA AND ISO EQUIVALENT CLASSIFICATIONS

The cabling systems specified in both TIA and ISO standards are intended to have a useful life of 10 years for Category 5_E and Category $6/6_A$ cables. However, the ISO/IEC Class F and Class F_A (also referred to as Category $7/7_A$) cables were meant to have a 15 years lifecycle.

LAN Cabling and Standards

There are two wiring schemes following the TIA/EIA-568 standard and used for UTP cabling; T-568A and T-568B, Figure 49.

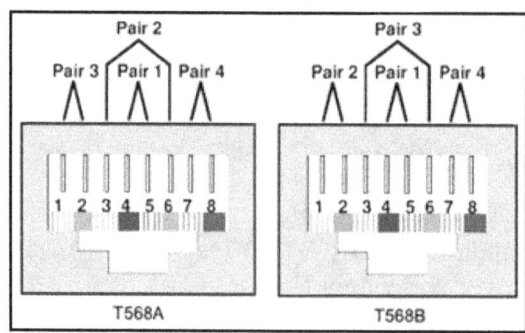

Figure 49: T-568A and T-568B Wiring Standards

Based on TIA/EIA-568-B.1-2001 standard, the T-568A and T-568B wiring schemes define the order of connections for UTP wires in 8P8C modular connector plugs and jacks.

The only difference between T-568A and T-568B is that the pin positions for the green and orange pairs have been switched.

T-568B was the most widely chosen wiring schematic in the US because it matches AT&T's old 258A color code. In addition, T568B offers backward compatibility with USOC standard.

T568B is, by now, a deprecated standard in the US and is no longer supported by TIA.

TIA/EIA recommends T-568A for new construction and is common in the rest of the world.

Straight-Through versus Crossover

Although there are 4 pairs of wires in a UTP cable, the 10BaseT and 100BaseT Ethernet standards use only 2 pairs for data signals: Orange and Green (Pairs 2 and 3), Table 7.

In T-568B for example, pair 2 is used to transmit data while pair 3 is used to receive data.

The other two colored pairs (Blue and Brown in pairs 1 and 4 respectively) may be used for a second Ethernet line, phone connections or Power over Ethernet (PoE) to supply DC power to IP phones, wireless access points, or video camera.

	T-568B			T-568A		
Pin	Pair	Color	Pin Name	Pair	Color	Pin Name
1	2	Orange Stripe	TX+	3	Green Stripe	RX+
2	2	Orange	TX-	3	Green	RX-
3	3	Green Stripe	RX+	2	Orange Stripe	TX+
4	1	Blue	Not Used	1	Blue	Not Used
5	1	Blue Stripe	Not Used	1	Blue Stripe	Not Used
6	3	Green	RX-	2	Orange	TX-
7	4	Brown Stripe	Not Used	4	Brown Stripe	Not Used
8	4	Brown	Not Used	4	Brown	Not Used

Table 7: T-568A and T-568B Pinouts

With the T-568B wiring scheme, the RJ-45 MDI (Medium Dependent Interface) socket or port on the NIC installed on a PC, transmits data over pin 1 and pin 2, and receives data over pin 3 and pin 6, Figure 50.

```
MDI RJ-45 Port
Pin    Label

1      TX+
2      TX-
3      RX+
4      NC
5      NC
6      RX-
7      NC
8      NC
```

Figure 50: MDI Pins Layout

On the other side, the RJ-45 MDI-X (Medium Dependent Interface with Cross-Over) port of an Ethernet switch, receives data over pin 1 and pin 2, and transmits data over pin 3 and pin 6, Figure 51.

```
MDI-X RJ-45 Port
Pin    Label

1      RX+
2      RX-
3      TX+
4      NC
5      NC
6      TX-
7      NC
8      NC
```

Figure 51: MDI-X Pins Layout

To connect two RJ-45 ports having different pin layouts; MDI and MDI-X, a straight through cable is required where each pin at one end of the cable connects to the same pin number at the other end of the cable. For example, pin 1 which is a Transmit at the PC end should connect to pin 1 which is a Receive at the Ethernet switch port end, and so on.
The two ends of the UTP cable should be implemented using the same wiring scheme; T-568A or T-568B, Figure 52.

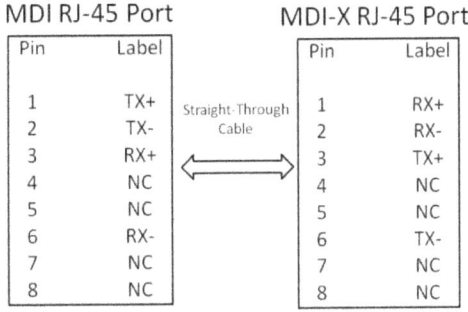

Figure 52: Connecting between MDI and MDI-X Ethernet Ports

If the two RJ-45 ports to be connected have the same pin layouts; MDI or MDI-X, then a crossover cable is required. For example with an Ethernet MDI port at both ends (PC to PC), pin 1 (Transmit) at one end should connect to pin 3 (Receive) at the other end and pin 3 (Receive) at one end should connect to pin 1 (Transmit) at the other end, as well, Figure 53.

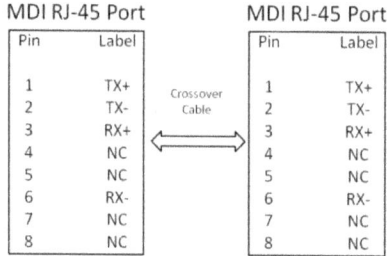

Figure 53: Connecting Two MDI Ethernet Ports

The MDI/MDI-X pinouts for 1GBASE-T and 10GBASE-T are illustrated in Figure 54.

MDI RJ-45 Port		MDI-X RJ-45 Port	
Pin	Label	Pin	Label
1	TX1+	1	TX2+
2	RX1-	2	RX2-
3	TX2+	3	TX1+
4	TX3+	4	TX4+
5	RX3-	5	RX4-
6	RX2-	6	RX1-
7	TX4+	7	TX3+
8	RX4-	8	RX3-

Figure 54: MDI/MDI-X Pins Layout for 1/10 Gigabit Ethernet

With the two wiring schemes, it is possible to create a cross-over cable with T-568A pinouts at one end and T-568B at the other end, or a straight-through cable with T-568B or T-568A standards at both ends), as depicted in Figure 55.

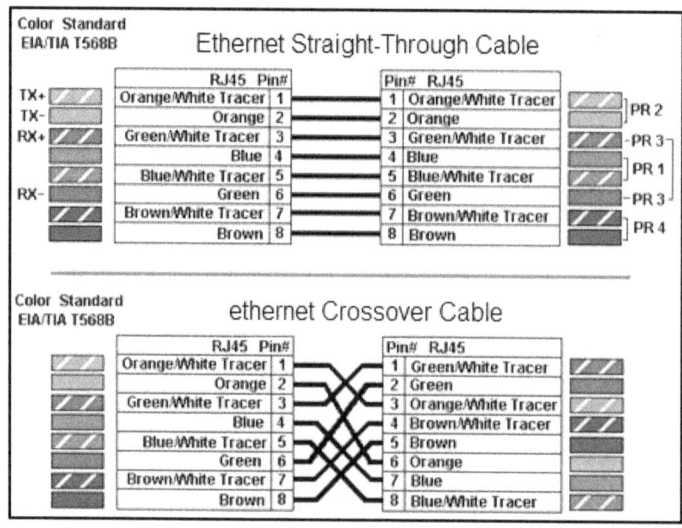

Figure 55: Straight-Through (above) and Cross-Over Cable (below) 10Base-T/100Base-T using EIA/TIA T568B Standard

Many commercial 10/100Base-T crossover cables seem not to cross pairs (4, 5) and (7, 8). This can be acceptable, since these pairs are not used, as depicted in Figure 56.

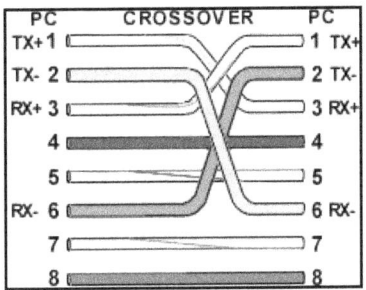

Figure 56: Pairs 4 and 5 not Crossed in 10/100 BASE-T Crossover

Crossed cables are now practically irrelevant for anything but older equipment. Modern devices such as Ethernet switches and Ethernet Network Interface Cards support the Auto MDI/MDI-X feature introduced in 1998 and used to detect the cable type. Nowadays, it is possible to use straight cables to connect two devices of the same type; a PC to a PC, a router to a router, or a switch to a switch - but when using older equipment at both ends, you may still need a crossover cable.

Terminating a Category 5/5$_E$/6 UTP Cable

The steps to build a Category 5/5E/6 UTP LAN cable are shown below:

1. Prepare Category 5, 5_E or 6 UTP cable. Make sure you choose the appropriate cable category based on you applications requirements. For example, for 100 Mbps, Category 5 and 5E will do the job although Category 5_E is the most suitable but it is obsolete by today's requirement.
   In you intend to run applications at higher speeds such as 1 Gbps then Category 6 should be used.

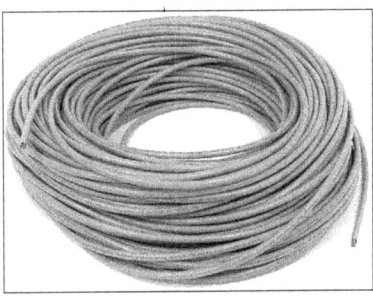

UTP Cable

2. Prepare new 8P8C RJ-45 connectors that will fit with the UTP cable. For example, if the UTP cable has stranded wire conductors then RJ-45 connectors for stranded wires should be used. The same is true with respect to solid wire conductors.

Also, the wires should fit correctly into the connector's pins according to the physical dimensions and diameters of the wires.

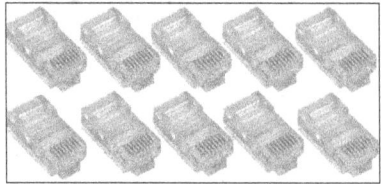

RJ-45 Plugs

3. Prepare cabling tools such as wire stripper, cable cutter and RJ-45 crimp tool in order to fix the RJ-45 connectors to both ends of the UTP cable.

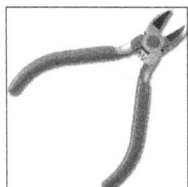

Wire Cutter

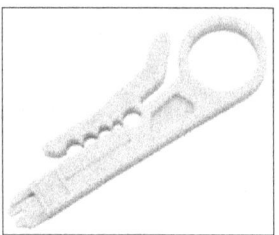

Cable Stripper

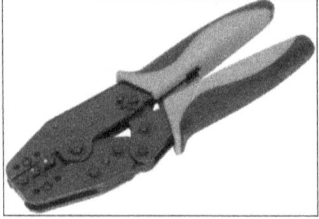

Crimp Tool

The appropriate choice of the crimp tool should be done depending on whether the cable wire conductors are stranded or solid. Crimp tools do exist to support both types of cable wire conductors.

4. Use the cable stripper tool to cut the UTP cable jacket at both ends of the cable.

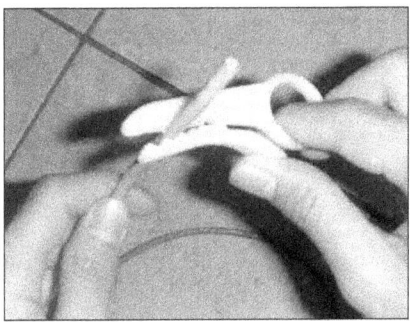

5. Cut into the plastic sheath 1" from the end of the cut cable.

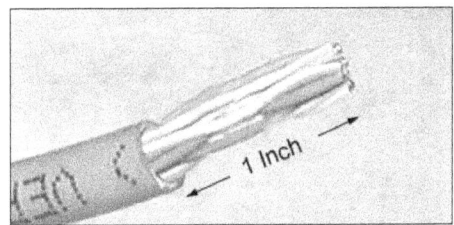

6. Unwind any pair of similar colors. The amount of untwisting in a pair as a result of termination to connecting hardware shall be no greater than 13 mm for category 5 cables (Category 5e as well).

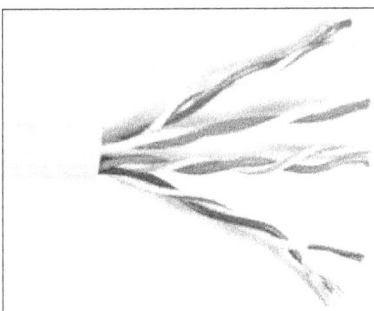

7. Pinch the wires between your fingers and straighten them out as shown.

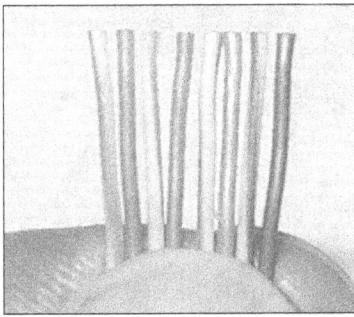

8. Use cutters to make a straight cut across the wires 13mm (½ inch) from the cut sleeve to the end of the wires.

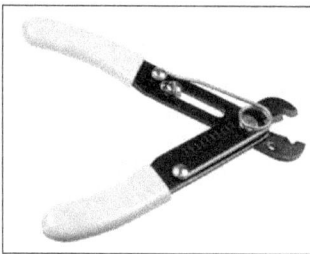

9. With the connector pins facing up, slide the wires into the connector. Insure that the wires are firmly seated to the end of the connector.

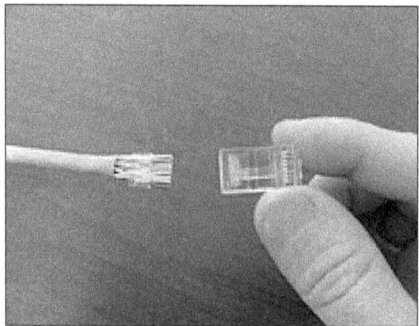

With Category 6 UTP cable, the RJ-45 plug with the same rating will come with a load bar. This small plastic piece is installed inside the plug before the wires are installed into the plug.

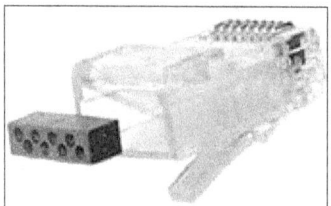

10. Push the wires into the connector.

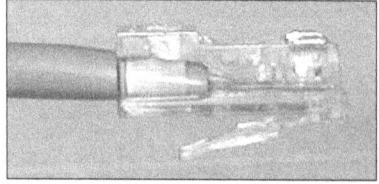

This is a view from the side. All the wires are firmly pushed and inserted into their respective connector tracks. In Category 5e, the twists of the wire pairs should be less than 13 mm (½ inch) to termination pins. In Category 6 and 6A, the twists should be closer to termination pins. The reason for making the twists as close to the termination as possible is to minimize crosstalk.

11. Place the connector into the crimp tool, and squeeze enough (not too hard) so that the handle reaches its full swing. If the connector is damaged due to high physical pressure with the crimping tool, the portion of the cable with the connector should be cut and the steps above should be repeated.

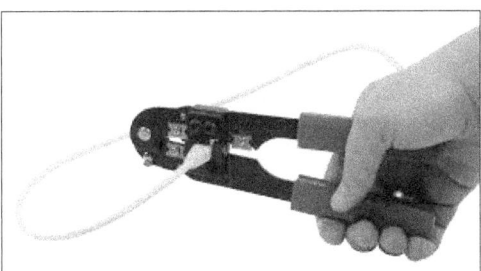

12. Always use a cable tester to check for continuity, opens and shorts.

Building a UTP LAN cable is not a difficult process. Usually, things will not work well during the first attempts. However after few practices, the chances of success will be there.

Terminating a Category 6A F/UTP Cable

Below, the steps to terminate a Category 6A F/UTP cable are as described in a blog[1] published on Wednesday, December 9, 2009:

---

[1] http://discountlowvoltage.blogspot.com/

Ethernet LAN Cables: For Computer Networks Professionals

1. Remove about 2 inches of the cable jacket.

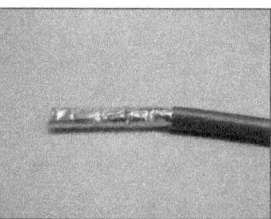

2. Cut off the outer plastic

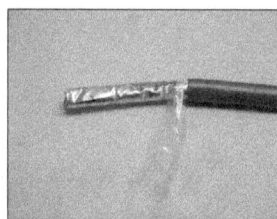

3. Pull back the foil and drain wire

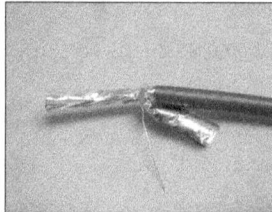

4. Cut off the inner plastic

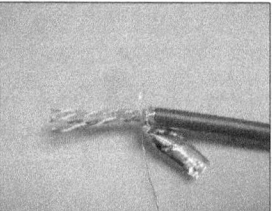

5. Leave about 0.25" of the foil and wrap it about the cable. Wrap the drain wire around the foil.

6. Pull back all four pairs of wires and cut off the spline

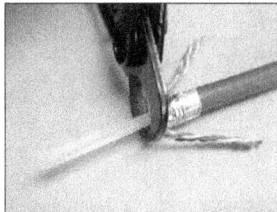

7. Untwist the wires and bring each wire to the appropriate slot according to the 568B wiring diagram

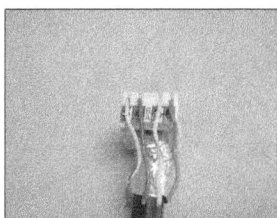

8. Cut of excess wires from the wires

9. Insert the cap into the Cat6A keystone jack. Notice that the jack and the cap have arrows on them. Make sure they are both pointing the same direction.

10. Close the jaw all the way until it clicks

11. If you are having trouble closing the jaw, open it back up and push down on both sides of the cap. This will seat the wires.

12. Now do the other side

13. Push the shielding lug up against the cable

14. Use a plier to get much tighter seal

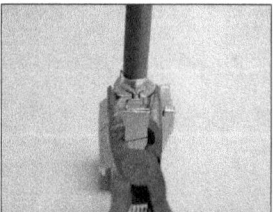

15. Install the included zip-tie to make sure nothing comes loose and you are done. This is a completed Cat6A shielded keystone jack.

Wire Map Test

Wire map test verifies that all eight wires are connected to the correct pins at both ends of the cable, Figures 57 and 58.

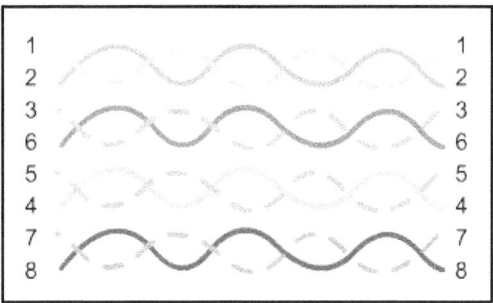

Figure 57: Correct T568B Wiring

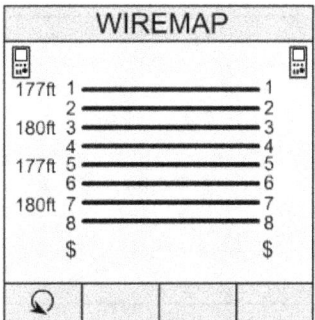

Figure 58: A Good Wiremap

The wire map test insures that the following problems do not exist on the cable:

1. Open: An open circuit occurs if the wire does not attach properly at the connector, Figure 59.

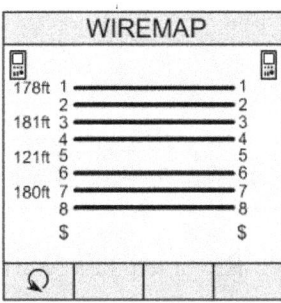

Figure 59: Open Circuit

2. Short: A short circuit occurs if two wires are connected to each other, Figure 60.

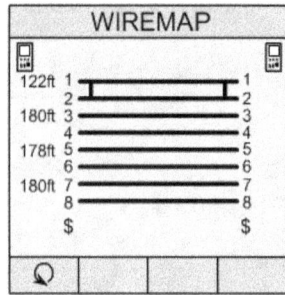

Figure 60: Short Circuit

3. Crossed pair: A wire pair is connected to completely different pins at both ends, Figure 61.

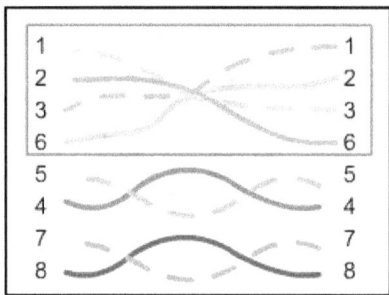

Figure 61: Crossed-Pair Wiring Fault

4. Reversed pair: A wire pair is correctly installed on one connector but reversed on the other connector, Figure 62.

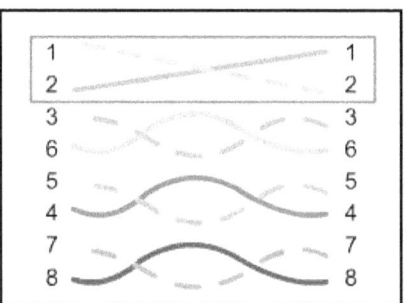

Figure 62: Reversed-Pair Wiring Fault

5. Split pair: Two wires from different wire pairs are connected to the wrong pins at both ends of the cable, Figure 63.

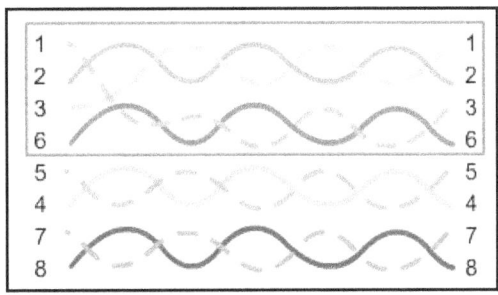

Figure 63: Split-Pair Wiring Fault

Attenuation

It is the decrease in signal amplitude over the length of a link, Figure 64. For testing, the highest frequencies that the cable is rated to support are used.
Ensuring minimal signal attenuation is critical because digital signal processing (DSP) technology cannot compensate for excessive signal loss.
Attenuation is expressed in (dB). Smaller dB values indicate better link performance.

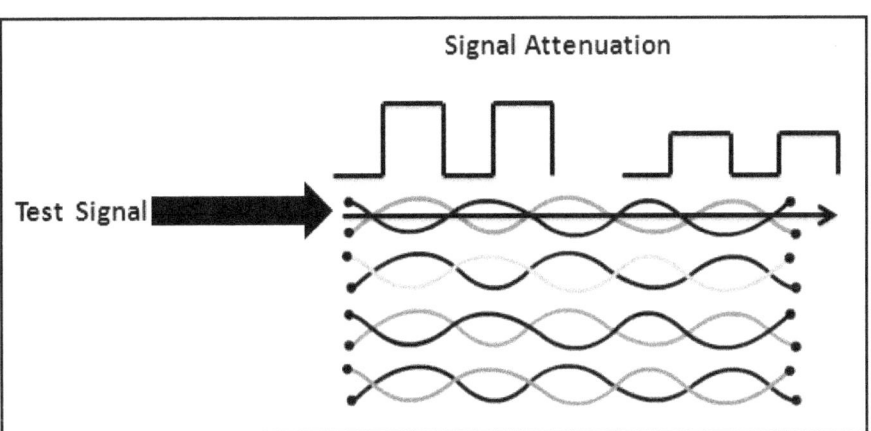

Figure 64: Signal Attenuation

In Table 8[2], Category 6 cables show better attenuation compared to Category 5e over 100 meters UTP runs for different frequencies. This is true especially for higher frequencies. Just by analyzing the attenuation values for 100 MHz frequency, it appears that Category 5e cables attenuate the signal transmitted in 22.0 dB while Category 6 cables attenuate the signal in 19.8 dB for this same frequency.

---
[2] Table 8 through Table 15 are sourced from http://www.siemon.com/uk/white_papers/04-01-15_cat6.asp

Frequency (MHz)	Category 5e solid UTP Cable Attenuation (dB)	Category 6 solid UTP Cable Attenuation (dB)
0.772	1.8	1.8
1.0	2.0	2.0
4.0	4.1	3.8
8.0	5.8	5.3
10.0	6.5	6.0
16.0	8.2	7.6
20.0	9.3	8.5
25.0	10.4	9.5
31.25	11.7	10.7
62.5	17.0	15.4
100.0	22.0	19.8
200.0	NA	29.0
250.0	NA	32.8

Table 8: Attenuation of Solid UTP Cable for Category 5e and 6 Over 100 m

Insertion Loss

The term *insertion loss* now replaces the *term attenuation*. The first started to be used as a replacement for the second in the standard documents to stress that the attenuation of the signal that propagates between a transmitter and a receiver in a communication system occurs due to the insertion of cable runs and connectors between them.

It is the combination of the effects of signal attenuation due to the cable length, resistance of the copper material, signal leaks through insulation of the cable, impedance caused by defective connectors, and impedance discontinuities due to connectors and patch panel installation, Figure 65.

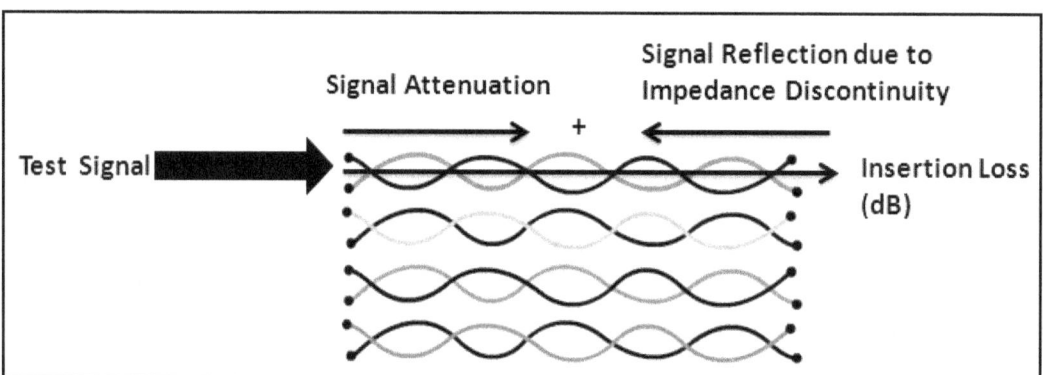

Figure 65: Insertion Loss Effect

In Table 9, Category 6 cables show better insertion loss compared to Category 5e for different frequencies.

Frequency (MHz)	Category 5e Channel (100 m) Insertion Loss (dB)	Category 6 Permanent Link (90 m) Insertion Loss (dB)
1.0	2.2	2.1
4.0	4.5	4.0
8.0	6.3	5.7
10.0	7.1	6.3
16.0	9.1	8.0
20.0	10.2	9.0
25.0	11.4	10.1
31.25	12.9	11.4
62.5	18.6	16.5
100.0	24.0	21.3
200.0	NA	31.5
250.0	NA	35.9

Table 9: Insertion Loss for Category 5e and 6 Channels

Impedance Discontinuity

It is caused by connectors having different impedance than the cable (For example the Category 5 cable has 100 Ohm impedance). This causes the signal to be reflected back to the transmitting device, Figure 66.

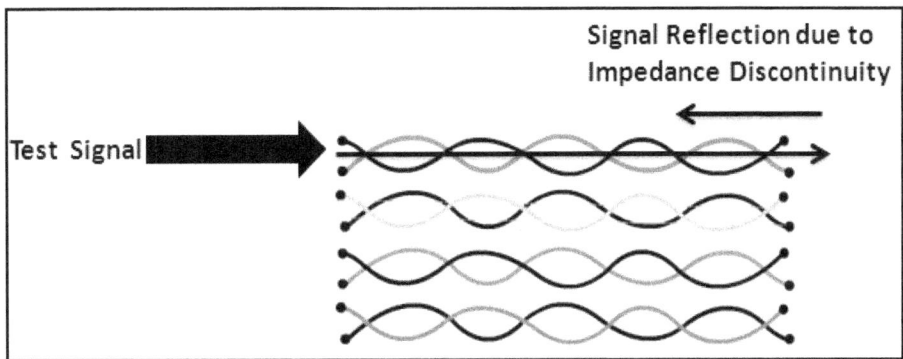

Figure 66: Impedance Discontinuity Effect

Return Loss

Return loss (also referred to as reflection loss) is a measure of the reflected energy from a transmitted signal due to a discontinuity in a wire. This reflected energy causes a reduction of the power of a transmitted signal at the receiver end.
The discontinuity can be a mismatch caused by connectors having different impedance than the cable or an improper installation of the cable and connectors in a channel, Figure 67.

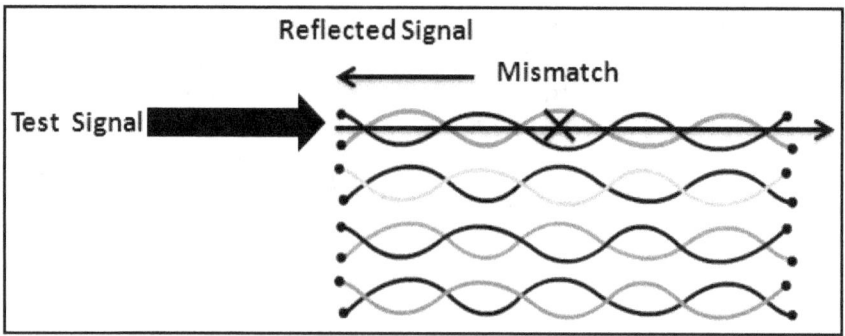

Figure 67: Return Loss Effect

In Table 10, the return loss values for both Categories 5e and 6 100-meter length cables are exactly the same up to 100-MHz frequency. This is because both cables have the same impedance of 100 ohms with the connecting hardware impedance for Category 5e and 6 being within the same range of values.

Frequency	Return Loss (dB)	Return Loss (dB)
1.0	20	20
4.0	23	23
8.0	24.5	24.5
10.0	25.0	25.0
16.0	25.0	25.0
20.0	25.0	25.0
25.0	24.3	24.3
31.25	23.6	23.6
62.5	21.5	21.5
100.0	20.1	20.1
200.0	NA	18.0
250.0	NA	17.3

Table 10: Return Loss values for Category 5e and 6 Solid UTP Cables

Connector Return Loss

It is the reflection or echo caused by impedance mismatches which occur when a high-speed signal enters or exits a connector.

Propagation Delay

It is the measurement of how long it takes for a signal to travel along the cable being tested. It is in the order of *ns*. If a signal, at one end of the link, is being transmitted at time t, it will reach the other end of the link at time $t+\Delta t$. The small increment Δt is the propagation delay that the signal takes to travel between the two ends of the link, Figure 68.

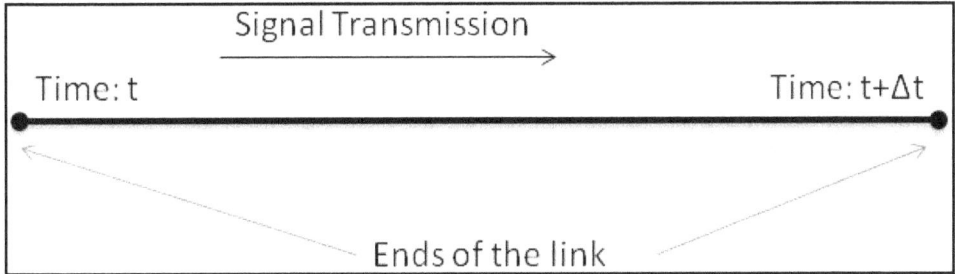

Figure 68: Propagation Delay through a Link

Time Domain Reflectometry

It measures the length of a wire based on the electrical delay. It is also used to identify the distance to the wiring fault.

A Time Domain Reflectometer (*TDR*) transmits an incident pulse along the conductor. When the incident pulse reaches a wiring fault or the other end of the link, a reflection of this pulse is sent back to the *TDR*, Figure 69.

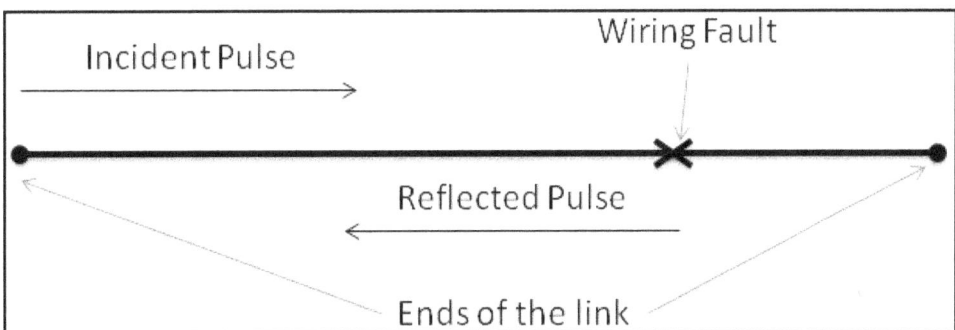

Figure 69: Time Domain Reflectometry

The reflection will have the same shape as the incident pulse, but the sign and magnitude depends on the change in impedance level of the link and the wiring fault.

By knowing the time it takes between when the incident pulse (t_i) is sent and its reflection is received (t_r); $T= t_r - t_i$ and the velocity of the electrical pulse on the conductor and which is closer to the speed of light; V, it is then possible to compute the distance D between the two ends of the link or between one end of the link and the wiring fault causing the reflection:

$$D = \frac{V \times T}{2}$$

Delay Skew

The propagation delays of different wires in a single cable can differ slightly because of the difference in the number of twists and electrical properties of each wire pair, Figure 70. If the delay skew between the pairs is too great, the bits arrive at different times and the data reassembly will be affected and delayed.

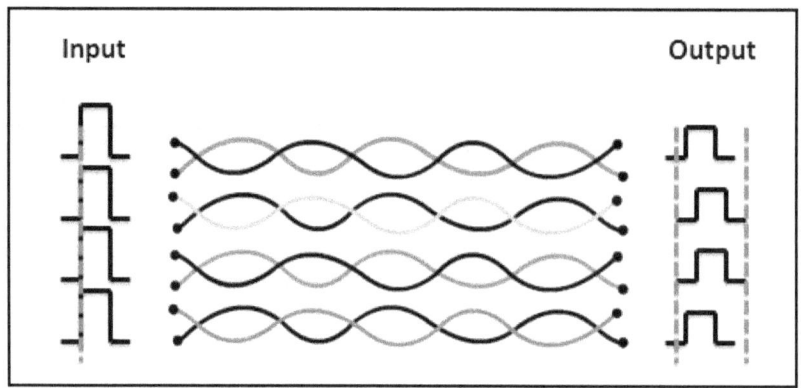

Figure 70: Delay Skew

Twisted Pair Cable Crosstalk

In network cabling, crosstalk refers to electromagnetic interference from one unshielded twisted pair to another unshielded twisted pair, running in parallel, Figure 71.

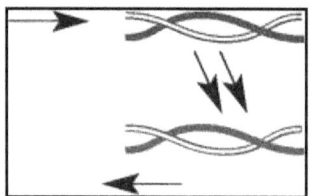

Figure 71: Crosstalk Signal

This phenomenon occurs when an electrical current or signal in one wire in a wire pair induces an unwanted electrical current or signal in another wire pair running in parallel.
The maximum bit rate which can be transmitted is limited by the crosstalk effects.

Near-End Cross-Talk - NEXT

A cable tester measures the NEXT value by applying a test signal to one cable pair and measuring the amplitude of the crosstalk signals received by the other cable pairs at the same end of the cable, Figure 72.

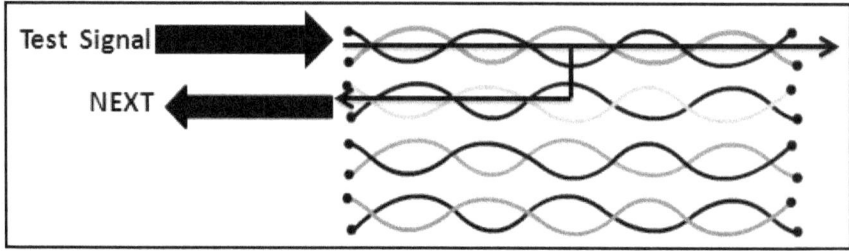

Figure 72: NEXT Effect

Table 11 shows the NEXT loss effect in dB for both Category 5e and Category 6 Solid UTP cables. Higher positive values for NEXT loss are better.

Frequency (MHz)	Pair-to-Pair NEXT Loss (dB) Category 5e Solid UTP Cable	Pair-to-Pair NEXT Loss (dB) Category 6 Solid UTP Cable
0.150	Not available	86.7
0.772	67.0	76.0
1.0	65.3	74.3
4.0	56.3	65.3
8.0	51.8	60.8
10.0	50.3	59.3
16.0	47.2	56.2
20.0	45.8	54.8
25.0	44.3	53.3
31.25	42.9	51.9
62.5	38.4	47.4
100.0	35.3	44.3
200.0	NA	39.8
250.0	NA	38.3

Table 11: Pair-to-Pair NEXT loss values for Category 5e and 6 UTP Cables

It is clear that Category 6 cables provide a better performance in regards to NEXT interference compared to Category 5e cables. An example is the NEXT loss values at 100 MHz frequency, which is 35.3 dB for Category 5e cables, and 44.3 dB for Category 6 cables.

Far-End Cross-Talk – FEXT

Due to attenuation, crosstalk occurring further away from the transmitter creates less noise on a cable than NEXT. This is called far-end crosstalk or FEXT, Figure 73.

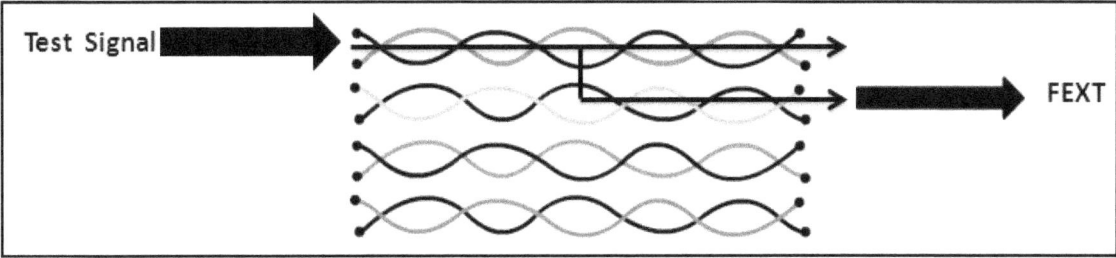

Figure 73: FEXT Effect

The noise caused by FEXT still travels back to the source, but it is attenuated as it returns. Thus the effect of FEXT is not as important as the one due to NEXT.

Power-Sum NEXT – PSNEXT

It measures the cumulative effect of NEXT from all wire pairs in the cable, Figure 74. PSNEXT is computed for each wire pair as the sum of the NEXT effect of the other three pairs.

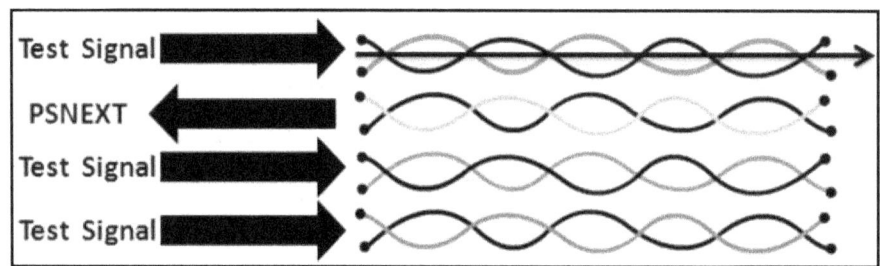

Figure 74: PSNEXT Effect

Table 12 indicates that Category 5e cables are more susceptible to Near End Crosstalk interference than Category 6 cables. For instance, the values of PSNEXT for both cables categories at a frequency of 100 MHz; for Category 6 cables the PS-NEXT loss is 42.3 dB and for Category 5e cables 32.3 dB. The same as for NEXT, higher positive values for PSNEXT loss are better.

Frequency (MHz)	PS-NEXT Loss (dB) Category 5e Solid Cable	PS-NEXT Loss (dB) Category 6 Solid Cable
0.150	74.7	84.7
0.772	64.0	74.0
1.0	62.3	72.3
4.0	53.3	63.3
8.0	48.8	58.8
10.0	47.3	57.3
16.0	44.2	54.2
20.0	42.8	52.8
25.0	41.3	51.3
31.25	39.9	49.9
62.5	35.4	45.4
100.0	32.3	42.3
200.0	NA	37.8
250.0	NA	36.3

Table 12: PSNEXT loss values for Category 5e and 6 UTP Cables

Attenuation to Crosstalk Ratio - ACR

This is the difference between the signal attenuation and near-end crosstalk (NEXT). It is measured in decibels and is a calculation used in networking transmissions in order to ensure that signals transmitted across twisted pair cables are stronger at the receiving end than interference signals imposed on the pair by crosstalk from adjacent pairs.

Attenuation and crosstalk must be minimized in order for acceptable signal transmission. Attenuation depends on the length and type of cable and as such cannot be changed. However, crosstalk can be minimized by making sure that the cables meet certain standards.
The ACR value is computed using the expression below:

$$ACR = Attenuation - NEXT \text{ (dB)}$$

In the presence of the near end crosstalk there is a risk that a higher-level signal on one pair disturbs an attenuated lower-level signal on another pair at the near end. This situation is shown in Figure 75, where the signal propagating to direction A causes NEXT crosstalk to the other pair carrying a signal in direction B.

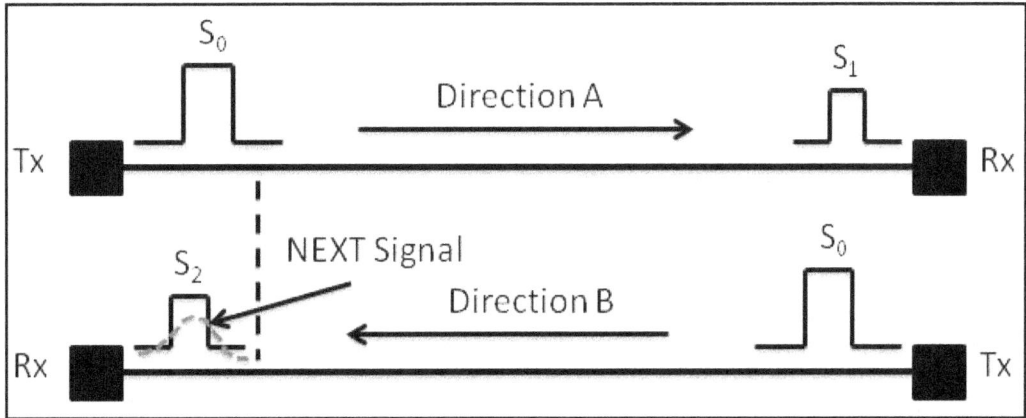

Figure 75: Attenuation to Crosstalk Ratio Effect

Positive ACR calculations mean that attenuated received signal strength is stronger than that of near-end crosstalk.
Negative ACR calculations mean that attenuated received signal strength is weaker than that of near-end crosstalk and is prone for corruption by the NEXT effect.

Power Sum Attenuation to Cross-Talk Ratio – PSACR

PSACR shows if the signal is strong enough to be detected over the noise when you are using all four pairs at one time.
PSACR is a calculation and is defined as the difference between PSNEXT and *attenuation*. PSACR is computed in the same way as ACR, but using the PSNEXT value in the calculation rather than NEXT:

$$PSACR = Attenuation - PSNEXT \text{ (dB)}.$$

Table 13 shows the PSACR performance between the Category 5e and Category 6.
The values of PSACR for both cables categories at a frequency of 100 MHz show Category 6 outperforming Category 5e cables. Higher positive values for PSACR are better.

Frequency (MHz)	Category 5e Channel PSACR (dB)	Category 6 Channel PSACR (dB)
1.0	54.8	59.9
4.0	46.0	56.5
8.0	39.3	49.9
10.0	36.9	47.7
16.0	31.5	42.6
20.0	28.8	40.0
25.0	25.9	37.2
31.25	22.8	34.3
62.5	12.0	24.1
100.0	3.1	15.8
200.0	NA	0.4
250.0	NA	-5.7

Table 13: PSACR response for Category 5e and 6 Channels

The same as for the ACR seen above, for positive PSACR value, the communication can be guaranteed. When the PSACR value is equal to zero, there is a state of uncertainty. For a negative PSACR value, the communication cannot be established at all.

Attenuation to Crosstalk Ratio, Far-End (ACRF) (previously known as Equal-Level FEXT loss)

ACRF is an ISO terminology expressed in dB as the difference between the measured FEXT and the attenuation of the wire pair whose signal is disturbed by the FEXT.
The *ACRF* crosstalk is computed using the expression below:

$$ACRF = Attenuation - FEXT \text{ (dB)}$$

Negative ACR calculations mean that attenuated received signal strength is weaker than that of FEXT and is prone for corruption by the FEXT effect.
Positive ACRF calculations mean that attenuated received signal strength is stronger than that of FEXT.
ACRF is critical, when more than one pair in the cable is used for high speed transmission in the same direction such as 1-Gigabit and 10-Gigabit Ethernet speeds.
Table 14 compares the ACRF values between Category 5e and Category 6 Solid UTP cables at different frequencies. The same as for PSACR, higher positive values for ACRF are better.

Frequency (MHz)	Pair-to-Pair ACRF (dB) Category 5e Solid UTP Cable (100 m)	Pair-to-Pair ACRF (dB) Category 6 Solid UTP Cable (100 m)
0772	Not available	70.0
1.0	63.8	67.8
4.0	51.8	55.8

8.0	45.7	49.7
10.0	43.8	47.8
16.0	39.7	43.7
20.0	37.8	41.8
25.0	35.8	39.8
31.25	33.9	37.9
62.5	27.9	31.9
100.0	23.8	27.8
200.0	NA	21.8
250.0	NA	19.8

Table 14: Pair-to-Pair ACRF values for Category 5e and 6 solid UTP Cables

The ACRF between the pairs of UTP cables reduces as the frequency increases, proving that, for high frequencies, the PSACR interference is more important. Also, Category 6 cables offer a greater protection from PSACR compared to Category 5e cables.

In any frequency within the range of interest, the PSACR value for Category 6 cables is higher than that for Category 5e cables at the same frequency.

Power Sum Attenuation to Crosstalk Ratio, Far-End (previously known as Power Sum ELFEXT loss)

It is the combined effect of ACRF from all wire pairs. It is computed as the sum result of the ACRF from all three other pairs to one pair. It is expressed in dB. PSACRF is critical, when all four pairs of the cable are used simultaneously in the same transmission direction as in 1-Gigabit and 10-Gigabit Ethernet speeds.

Table 15 compares the PSACRF values between Category 5e and Category 6 channels at different frequencies. Again as before, higher positive values for PSACRF loss are better.

Frequency (MHz)	Pair-to-Pair PSACRF (dB) Category 5e Channel	Pair-to-Pair PSACRF (dB) Category 6 Channel
0772	NA	NA
1.0	54.4	60.3
4.0	42.4	48.2
8.0	36.3	42.2
10.0	34.4	40.3
16.0	30.3	36.2
20.0	28.4	34.2
25.0	26.4	NA
31.25	24.5	30.4
62.5	18.5	24.3
100.0	14.4	20.3
200.0	NA	14.2
250.0	NA	12.3

Table 15: PSACRF Loss values for Category 5e and 6 Channels

The PSACRF behavior is similar to the PSACR. All pairs are contributing to the PSACR interference ratios.

Alien Cross-Talk

The impact of Alien crosstalk has become obvious since 10-Gigabit Ethernet speeds have been widely used in data centers.

Alien crosstalk is also known as inter-line crosstalk. It describes the signal coupling between different cables in a bundle.

The largest impact of alien crosstalk comes from the so-called *six-around-one* or *six-surround-one* situation, Figure 76.

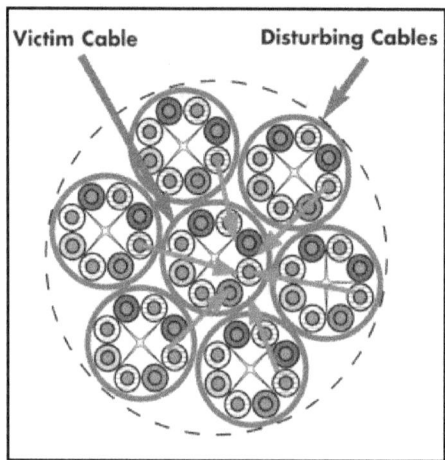

Figure 76: Alien Crosstalk

Each wire pair of the victim cable is subject to the EMI caused by high speed data signals flowing in the twenty four (6 cables x 4 wire pairs=24) wire pairs of the surrounding cables.
ANEXT is a measured quantity instead of a calculated one and the measurement will require 24 times 4 wire pairs of the victim cable, that is, 96 individual measurements.
For each wire pair of the victim cable, a signal is injected in each wire pair of the surrounding cables and the same process is repeated for the remaining wire pairs of the same victim cable.
The ANEXT measurement process is by itself lengthy for a single cable and definitely very lengthy if applied to all cables in a bundle.
The elimination of ANEXT is not possible using DSP noise cancelling techniques because the receiving hardware has no idea what data is being sent on the neighboring cable.

The amount of ANEXT effect depends on the following:

1. Type of cable.
2. Cable jacket.
3. Cable length.
4. Cable twists density.
5. Proximity of adjacent cables and connectors.
6. EMI/RFI external disturbance.

The Alien crosstalk in a Category 6 UTP cable is extremely dependent upon installation practices. However, it is significantly reduced when using the Category 6 F/UTP shielded cable.

In Category 6_A cables, crosstalk and ANEXT is minimized using tighter wires pairs twists.

The worst case scenario happens with Category 6_A cables tightly bundled. In this situation, the center cable will be affected heavily by the surrounding cables.

To reduce or minimize the ANEXT effect, one solution consists to unbundle and lay the cables loose in pathways and trace-ways with space between them.

This space will help reduce or minimize the coupling problems that affect two cables with high speed signals and running in parallel.

Also, the cables should be kept separated as far as possible at the back of the patch panels. To achieve this, screened patch leads should be used.

Since the category 6_A O.D is larger than the Category 6 O.D, the space between pairs in adjacent cables is reduced and this also reducing the capacitive or coupling effect (crosstalk) between channel signals. However, Category 6_A UTP is still affected by the ANEXT phenomenon.

There are two types of Alien cross-talks:

1. Alien Near End Cross-Talk – ANEXT - This phenomenon occurs between 2 adjacent channels or cables; a receiver (RX2) in one channel receives a power signal coupled from the transmitter (TX1) of another channel on the same side, Figure 77.

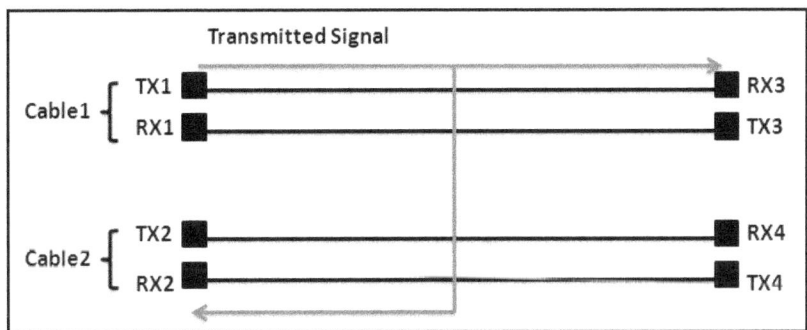

Figure 77: ANEXT Effect

2. Alien Attenuation to Cross-Talk at Far End (AACRF) - This other phenomenon occurs when the receiver RX4 at one side of a channel receives a signal power coupled from the transmitter TX1 at the other side of another channel, Figure 78.

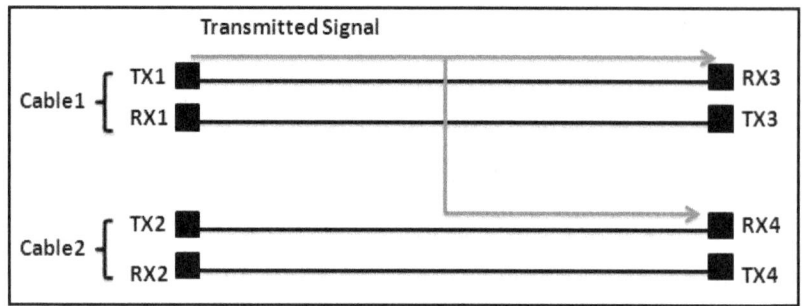

Figure 78: AACRF Effect

To avoid or reduce the effect of the ANEXT:

1. Use of shielded cables such as F/UTP and S/FTP.
2. Integrate shielded equipment.
3. Choose non-adjacent patch panels.
4. Avoid EMI/RFI areas.
5. Separate equipment cords.
6. Unbundling horizontal cables.

Power Sum ANEXT

Power Sum Alien Cross-Talk measured at the near-end is called power sum alien near-end crosstalk loss (**PS-ANEXT** loss)

PS-ANEXT sums four individual near end alien crosstalk measurements from each pair of the disturbing cable to a single pair of the disturbed cable, Figure 79.

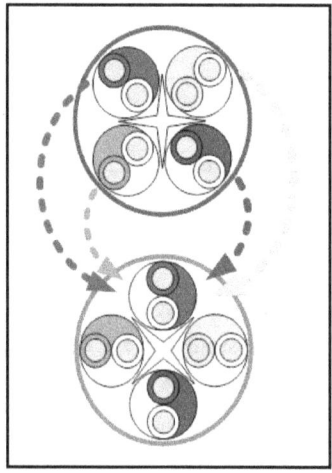

Figure 79: PS-ANEXT Effect

Power Sum Alien Attenuation to Crosstalk Ratio Far – PS-AACRF (previously known as Power Sum Equal-Level FEXT or PS-AELFEXT)

Power sum alien crosstalk measured at the far-end is called power sum alien attenuation to crosstalk ratio, far-end (**PS-AACRF**).

PS-AACRF sums four individual far end alien crosstalk measurements from each pair of the disturbing cable to a single pair of the disturbed cable.

As DSP technology advanced, NEXT, FEXT, and Return Loss could be filtered on a considerable basis.

The alien crosstalk that cannot be eliminated through active means has become the largest problem in confining the signal-to-noise ratio.

Performance Comparison Chart

Table 16[3] provides comparative channel performance data at 100 MHz for category 5_E/class D, category 6/class E, category 6_A/class E_A, class F, and class F_A channels.

	Category 5_E / Class D	Category 6 / Class E	Category 6_A / Class EA	Class F	Class FA
Frequency	1 – 100	1 - 250	1 - 500	1 - 600	1 – 1,000
Insertion Loss	24.0	21.3	20.9	20.8	20.3
NEXT Loss (dB)	30.1	39.9	39.91	62.9	65.0
PS-NEXT Loss	27.1	37.1	37.11	59.9	62.0
ACR (dB)	6.1	18.6	18.6	42.1	46.1
PS-ACR (dB)	3.1	15.8	15.8	39.1	41.7
ACRF (dB)	17.4	23.3	23.3	44.4	47.4
PS-ACRF (dB)	14.4	20.3	20.3	41.4	44.4
Return Loss	10.0	12.0	12.0	12.0	12.0
PS-ANEXT Loss	n/s	n/s	60.0	n/s	67.0
PS-AACRF (dB)	n/s	n/s	37.0	n/s	52.0
Propagation	548	548	548	548	548
Delay Skew (ns)	50	50	50	30	30

Table 16: INDUSTRY STANDARDS PERFORMANCE COMPARISON AT 100 MHZ FOR CHANNELS

Flat Ethernet Cable

In recent years, flat Ethernet cables have been proposed by many vendors, Figure 80.

Figure 80: Flat Ethernet Cable

---

[3] Table 16 is sourced from http://www.siemon.com/uk/white_papers/07-03-01-demystifying.asp

These cables have 8 wires and require RJ-45 connectors to connect Ethernet networking equipment. The wires, inside these cables, are not twisted like in the standard Ethernet LAN cables. This is mainly because most residential areas where these cables are supposed to be deployed are not faced with EMI problems, Figure 81 and Figure 82.

Figure 81: Bootless Flat Ethernet Cables

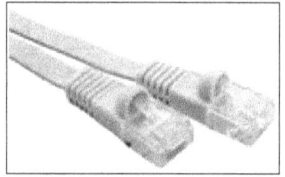

Figure 82: Flat Ethernet Cable with Snagless Boot

Ethernet cables are known to be subject to EMI and external noise. Using flat Ethernet cables for long runs is generally a bad idea.
For this reason, the flat Ethernet cables proposed by the vendors are limited to a maximum of 30 meters (100 ft), as observed through many vendors web sites. However, it should be mentioned that an insulation wrap for each pair is used by some cable vendors to protect against crosstalk for speed networks, as depicted in Figure 83.

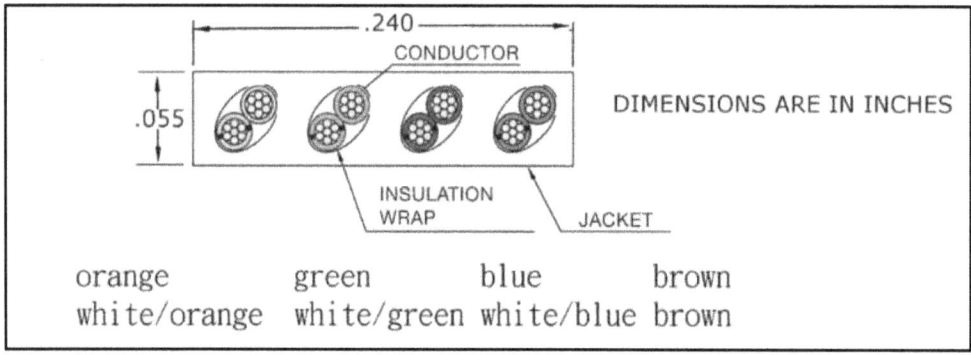

Figure 83: Insulation Wrap inside the Flat Ethernet Cable

Various flat Ethernet cables exist to support different categories (Category 3, 5, 5e, and 6) and classes (Class C, D, D_A, E, E_A) based on TIA/EIA and ISO/IEC specification standards, respectively.
They also support IEEE Ethernet protocols such as 10BASE-T, 100 BASE-T, 1GBASE-T and 10GBASE-T.
These cables are most of the time proposed in short runs and are ideal for hiding under carpets or running under doors.

Power over Ethernet – PoE

Power over Ethernet has been implemented in many variations before IEEE standardized 802.3af (2003). IEEE 802.3af specifies the ability to supply an endpoint device with 48V DC at up to 350mA or approximately 16.8W at a maximum (100 m) runs on category 5, 5e and 6 cables.
IEEE 802.3at (2009) updates the PoE standard to include support for Gigabit Ethernet LANs and splits systems into two categories based on the cable type:

1. Type 1 covers Cat5 cables and remains restricted to the IEEE 802.3af limits.
2. Type 2 covers Cat5 and Cat6 cables and supplies up to 600mA or approximately 28.8W. It is often referred to as PoE+.

The device must be capable of receiving power on either the data pairs [*Mode A*] (phantom power) or the unused pairs in 10BASE-T/100Base-T [*Mode B*], Figure 84.

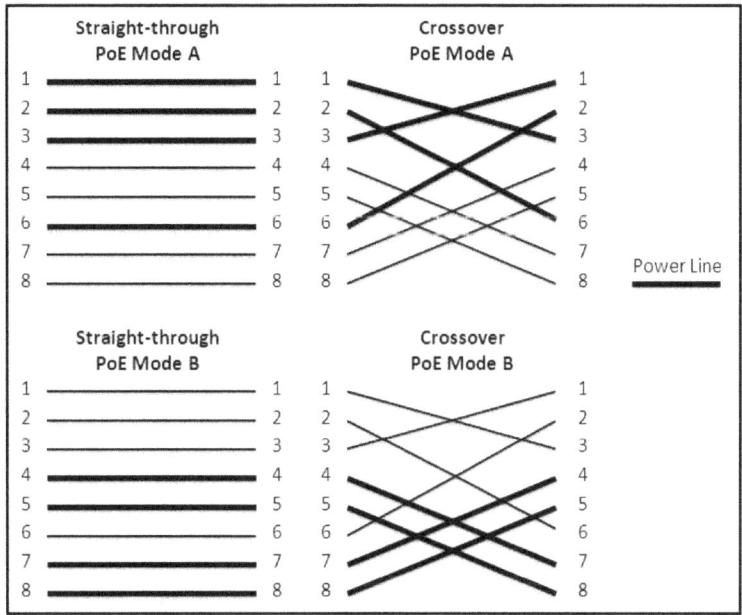

Figure 84: PoE over 10BaseT and 100BaseT Cables

In 10Base-T and 100Base-T, *Mode-A* PoE can be used on data wires and *Mode-B* PoE on the unused wires. This is true for both straight-through and cross-over cables.

Power is only supplied when a valid PoE endpoint is detected by using a low voltage probe to look for the PoE signature on the other endpoint.

In 1-Gbps Ethernet, PoE is used in *Mode-A* only because all 8 wires carry data. This is true for both straight-through and cross-over cables, Figure 85.

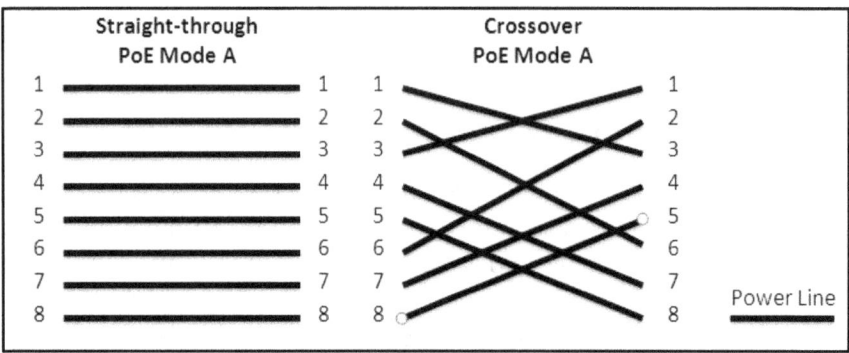

Figure 85: PoE Over Cables with Support of 1/10 Gbps Ethernet

PoE feature is very useful when providing power to devices such as IP phones, Wireless Access Points, and IP security cameras.

The effect of current limitation is to reduce heat in the wire and avoid damaging the powered device.

Cable Fire Rating

The behavior of the electric cables in case of fire can be evaluated according to various aspects:

1. Fire resistance: It can be considered as **active** since the cable continues to transmit power and signals even during the fire for a specific period of time (from 30 to 180 minutes).
2. Non propagation of fire and emission of fumes and acid gases: It can be defined as **passive**, but of primary importance, by limiting the fire propagation and by reducing fumes and gases that are developed by the combustion and that cause severe damages and human lives losses. It must be considered, in fact, that most commonly identified causes for death from a fire incident are due to gas or smoke.

Plenum Grade

In building construction, the plenum is the space that is used for air circulation in heating and air conditioning systems, typically between the structural ceiling and the suspended ceiling or under a raised floor.

Plenum cable is run in the plenum spaces of buildings. The plenum space is typically used to house the communication cables for the buildings computer and telephone network(s). However, use of plenum areas for cable deployment poses a serious hazard in the event of a fire as once the fire reaches the plenum space there are few barriers to contain the smoke and flames. Plenum cable is coated with fire-retardant coating, low smoke materials such as polyvinyl chloride (PVC), fluorinated ethylene polymer (FEP), or a polyolefin. These plastics offer good resistance against fire, and in the event that they do begin to burn, they will not emit large quantities of harmful fumes.

Riser cable

Cable that is to be run between floors in non-plenum areas is rated as riser cable. The fire requirements on riser cable are not as strict. Thus, plenum cable can always replace riser cable, but riser cable cannot replace plenum cable in plenum spaces.

Both plenum and riser cables commonly include a rope or polymer filament with high tensile strength, helping to support the weight of the cable when it is dangling in an open chute. Cables like twisted-pair are available in both plenum and riser versions.

The cable cost is often significantly higher than general-use cable, due to the special restricted-use flame retardant materials.

LSZH (Low Smoke Zero Halogen)

In a fire, a halogen-containing plastic material releases hydrogen chloride, a poisonous gas that forms hydrochloric acid when it comes in contact with water.

Designated halogen-free cables, on the other hand, do not produce a dangerous gas/acid combination or toxic smoke when exposed to flame.

The term LSZH indicates materials that are properly formulated to guarantee, besides the high self-extinguishing characteristic, also a low emission of clear fumes, without halogens (corrosive gases) when exposed to high sources of heat and that do not develop toxic gases in case of combustion.

This type of material is typically used in poorly ventilated areas such as aircraft or rail cars. It is also used extensively in the railroad industry, wherever high voltage or track signal wires must be run into and through underground tunnel systems. This reduces the chance of toxic gasses accumulating in these areas should the wires be damaged by fire or a short circuit fault.

Low smoke zero halogen is becoming very popular and, in some cases, a requirement where the protection of people and equipment from toxic and corrosive gas is critical.

Other benefits of halogen free cable include the fact that it is often lighter, so overall cable network system weights can be reduced. Also, the environmental impact of halogen free cabling can be lower if there are fewer toxic chemicals.

Summary about Copper Cables

Copper cabling in computer networking has a lifespan of 10 years as a minimum and 20 years as a maximum. It represents a non-negligible portion of the total cost of a LAN and constitutes a very important initial investment.

The choice of a good cabling system is very important to help reduce downtime periods and maintenance work and provide better network performance.

When it comes to buy a cable, the choice of a long-term solution is always brought to the front as one of the main aspects for consideration.

Other parameters should also be integrated in the choice of the cabling system such as:

1. Type of network applications to run over the cable (data, audio, videos), distance between different networked devices to be connected in a LAN.

2. The cable routing and whether it should be deployed through areas which necessitate special manipulations such as bending.
3. The already existing cables in place that should not constitute a degrading factor for newer cables to be deployed (for example, deploy a Category 6_A cable along with an already existing Category 5_E cable platform to support 10 Gbps speed is a bad idea).
4. The existence of an EMI external source that may require the use of shielded cables.
5. Fire hazards with all problems that can result.
6. Cost of the overall copper cabling solution including cables and hardware connectors, patch panel, cable conduit, etc…

Advantages of Copper

The main advantages of copper, when choosing a LAN cable for network connectivity are summarized below:

1. Copper cables use low cost connectors and transceivers.
2. Copper cables are cheaper compared to other solutions.
3. In the current state of technology, copper cabling support high speed LAN communication such as 10, 40 and 100 Gbps.
4. Copper cables are used in all networks and are very well known by all network professionals. Also, they are relatively easy to implement with simple tools except for higher speed grades where special care should be taken.

Disadvantages of Copper

On the other side, the copper cables have some disadvantages some of which are mentioned below:

1. Although power consumption has been reduced, it is still high around 5 W per port compared to other solutions.
2. The density of connectors for copper wires, compared to other solutions is low. This is especially true for the higher speed copper wires which use shielded connectors with relatively larger size compared to their unshielded counterpart.
3. Crosstalk and Interference are still the two biggest problems faced by copper cables systems.
4. Testing the cables to make sure it meets requirements and certifications is a long process; this is true especially when testing a cabling system for Alien Crosstalk.
5. Higher speed copper cables are more difficult and require more skills and training to install and deploy.

Ethernet LAN Fiber Optic Cable

An electrical current flowing through a copper wire generates a magnetic field. This magnetic field can leak out signals and hence information carried out by the copper wire.

Using a shielded copper wire such as STP cable or Coaxial cable can reduce the problem; however the shielding cannot stop the signal leak completely.

Optical fibers do not radiate any magnetic field and are immune to EMI since signals are transmitted as light instead of electrical current. Thus, they can carry signals through places where EMI would affect transmission.

The fiber optic cables support longer cable runs than copper and offer speeds such as 10 Mbps, 100 Mbps, 1 Gbps, 2.5 Gbps, 10 Gbps, 40 Gbps, and 100 Gbps, immunity to EMI, and low attenuation loss over long distances.

It should be noted that while with the coaxial cable the signal loss depends on frequency, this is not the case with the fiber optic cable.

In ordinary environments, it is not practical to use fiber optics to transmit data between personal computers and printers as it is too costly.

Fiber Optic cables transmit a digital signal via pulses of light (Laser or Infrared) through a very thin strand of glass. At the other end, the fiber cable is plugged into a receiver which decodes the optical signal back into digital pulses.

Fiber strands (the core of the fiber optic cable) are extremely thin, no thicker than a human hair, Figure 1. The core is surrounded by a cladding with lower index of refraction and which reflects the light back into the core and prevents light from escaping the cable.

Figure 1: Fiber Optic Cable

Optical Fiber Basics

Optical fibers typically include a transparent core surrounded by a transparent cladding material with a lower index of refraction. Light is kept in the *core* by total internal reflection. This causes the fiber to act as a waveguide, Figure 2.

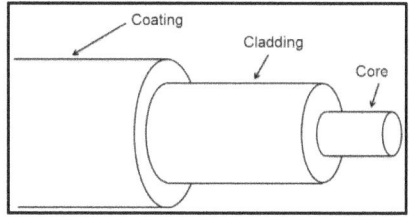

Figure 2: Fiber Optic Structure

The *core* is made of ultra-pure silica or glass and is the means of transmitting the light pulses through the cable from the transmitter to the receiver. It has a high reflective index.
The *cladding* material is of a different glass material and prevents the light from escaping the core, Figure 3.

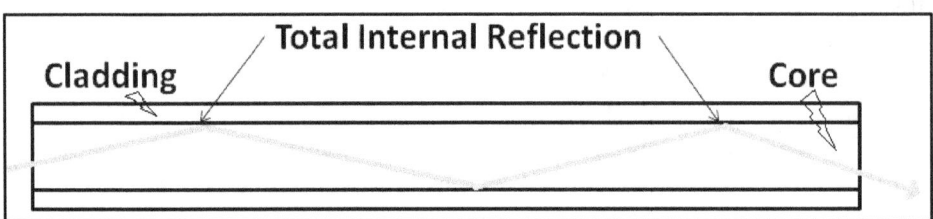

Figure 3: Total Internal Reflection

The *cladding* is surrounded with a protective plastic cover called the *coating* that protects the fiber from moisture and other damage.
The *core*, *cladding* and *coating* are specified using slashes (/) to separate the values of the diameters. For example, 50/125/250 means the core is 50 µm, the cladding is 125 µm and the *coating* is 250 µm. A short way of specifying the fiber is to only list the core and cladding sizes (50/125).
Hundreds or thousands of these optical fibers are arranged in bundles in optical cables. The bundles are protected by the cable's outer covering, called a *jacket*.

Mode Field

Some fibers can support *cladding modes* in which light propagates in the core as well as in the cladding. The *mode field* is the distribution of light through the *core* and *cladding* of a particular fiber.

Simplex versus Duplex Fiber Optic Cables

Simplex cable consists of a single fiber optic fiber or strand. Data is transmitted in one direction, transmit to receive. Duplex cable consists of two fiber optic strands, Figure 4.

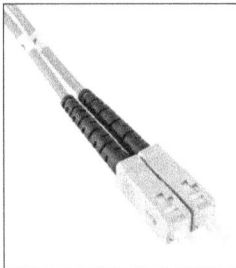

Figure 4: Duplex Fiber Optic Cable

One strand goes from transmit to receive and the other strand connects receive to transmit. This allows bi-directional communication between devices.

Single-Mode versus Multi-Mode Optical Fiber

When an LED light source produces a pulse of light entering the core at a particular angle, it produces light rays that travel down a finite number of paths through the core. These paths are called MODES. In other words, modes can be thought of as bundles of light rays of the same wavelengths entering the fiber at a specific angle.

Fibers that support many propagation paths or transverse modes are called multi-mode fibers (MMF), while those that only support a single propagation path are called single-mode fibers (SMF).

MMFs generally have a wider core diameter and are used for short-distance communication links and for applications where high power must be transmitted.

SMFs have a narrower core diameter and are used for long-haul network connections.

Single-Mode Operation

SMFs cables have a smaller core diameter of around 9 μm (usually 8.3 μm) and are used in network connections over long distances, Figure 5.

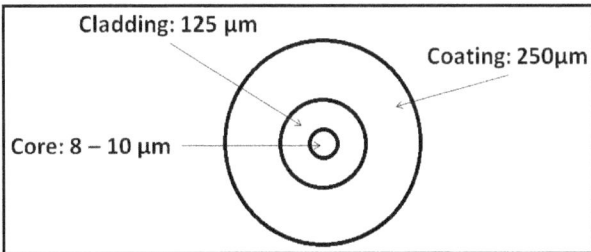

Figure 5: Single Mode Core

SMFs allow a single mode and pathway of light to travel through the core, as depicted in Figure 6.

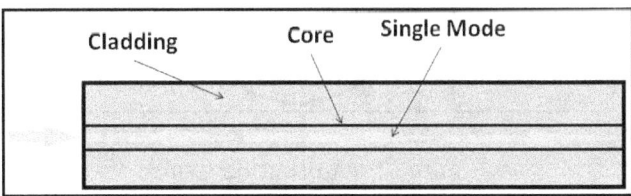

Figure 6: Single mode through the Core

It should be noted that, in general, the core diameter in a single mode fiber can range from 5 μm to 10 μm.

In the real world there are some additional issues for the cable designer to consider. As much as 20% of the light in a single-mode cable actually travels down the cladding. The effective diameter of the cable is a blend of the single-mode core and the degree to which the cladding carries light. This is referred to as the mode field diameter and it may be larger than the physical diameter of the core.

SMFs have the advantages of high information-capacity carrying, low attenuation, and low fiber cost.

SMF cable allows communication distances of between 40km and 200km as compared with as little as 2km for MMF. The superior capabilities of a single-mode fiber result from very precise manufacturing techniques. Because the telephone companies use SMF in large quantities, the cost per meter for SMF is actually lower than the MMF.

The beam of light used with SMFs must be from high quality laser light source and provide low attenuation. Generally, lower attenuations and higher bandwidths happen at longer wavelengths. For this reason, the most common wavelengths used with SMFs are 1310 nm and 1550 nm. However, Modern SMFs have low attenuation even at 850 nm wavelength.

It should be noted that a SMFs do not suffer from modal dispersion, modal noise, and other effects that come with multimode transmission. Signals are carried at higher speeds than multimode fibers throughout longer distances. However, the components and equipment are more expensive than their multimode counterparts.

SMFs are more fragile and need more protection (coating material) to make it manageable. This requires more manufacturing costs to support much higher bandwidth and larger distances. For these reasons, SMFs are commonly used for inter-building connectivity or WANs.

Multimode Operation

MMFs have a larger core diameter compared to SMFs, Figure 7. The first MMFs used in LANs had a core diameter of 62.5 µm with 125 µm diameter in cladding. In current days, MMFs with core diameters 50 µm and 100 µm diameter in cladding have been adopted. Still the core diameter of MMFs is almost 6 to 7 times wider than that of SMFs.

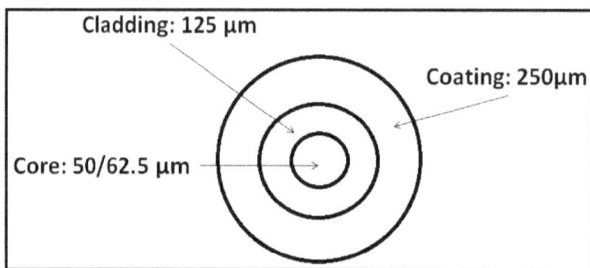

Figure 7: Multimode Core

The large core diameter of MMFs allows multiple pathways or modes and several wavelengths of light to be transmitted, Figure 8.

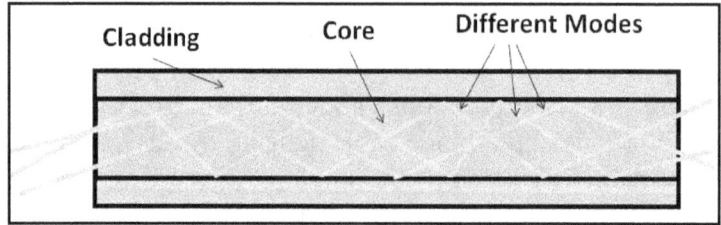

Figure 8: Multiple Modes through the Core

Some of the modes are longer than others. The light pulse will be spread out due to modal dispersion. This restricts the distance that a pulse can be usefully sent over multimode fiber.
As a cable length increases, the spread of a pulse increases. The light of the longer path falls further and further behind the light on the shortest path as the overall distance travelled increases. If the length of the MMF goes beyond a certain limit, then the pulses will overlap making the light signals at the receiving end totally unrecognizable.
For a multimode fiber with a core diameter of 62.5 microns, a light with a wavelength of 1300 nm will find roughly 228 modes for propagation.
Multimode fiber is commonly used in LAN backbones within buildings, patch cable applications such as fiber to the desktop or patch panel to equipment.
Multimode fiber, in spite of its shorter distance capabilities, is much better suited to carry the less focused light from a low-cost light emitting diode (LED). The LED is not as powerful as the laser, and the multimode fiber is potentially more expensive than the SMF used with the laser - but the LED transmitter device may be significantly less expensive than the laser transmitter device.

Graded-Index and Step-Index Fiber

Multi-mode optical fiber comes in either graded index or step index. The advantage of the graded index compared to step index is the considerable decrease in modal dispersion as depicted in Figure 9.

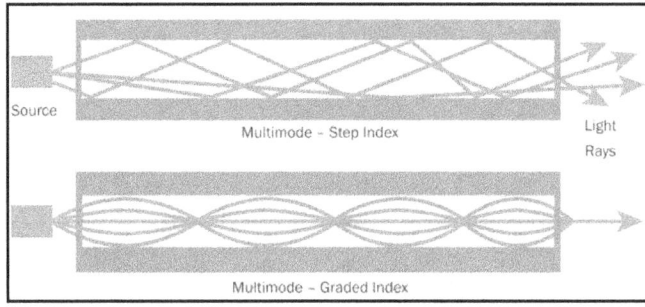

Figure 9: Step-Index and Graded-Index MMFs

Graded-Index Fiber

In fiber optics, a graded-index or gradient-index fiber is an optical fiber whose core has a refractive index that decreases with increasing radial distance from the optical axis of the fiber.
In other words, the refractive index of the core of the graded-index fiber is at maximum at the center of the core and then it decreases towards core-cladding interface.
Because parts of the core closer to the fiber axis have a higher refractive index than the parts near the cladding, light rays follow sinusoidal paths down the fiber, Figure 10.

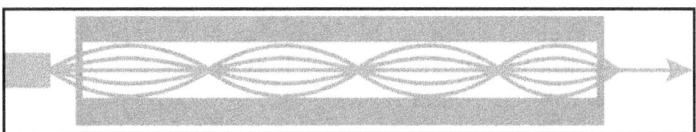

Figure 10: Graded-Index Multimode Fiber

This design compensates for modal dispersion by allowing light rays in the outer zones of the core to travel faster than those in the center of core.

The shortened path and the higher speed allow light at the periphery to arrive at a receiver at about the same time as the slow but straight rays in the core axis. The result: digital pulse suffers less dispersion. This type of fiber is best suited for local-area networks.

Different light modes in a graded-index multimode fiber still follow different lengths along the fiber.

However their speeds differ because the speed of guided light changes with fiber core's refractive index.

So the farther the light goes from the center of the fiber, the faster its speed. So the speed difference compensate for the longer paths followed by the light rays that go farthest from the center of the fiber. This equalizing of transit times of different modes greatly reduces modal dispersion.

It should be noted that modal dispersion may be considerably reduced, but never completely eliminated.

Graded-index fibers are commonly used in multimode fibers for data communications and networks carrying signals for moderate distances - typically no more than a couple of kilometers.

Step-Index Fiber

Step-index fibers have a uniform core with one index of refraction, and a uniform cladding with a smaller index of refraction, Figure 11.

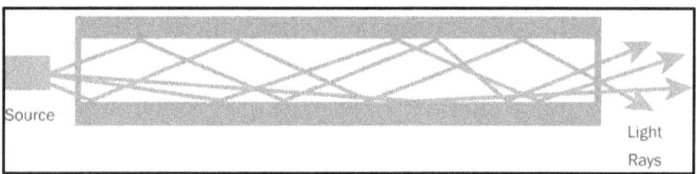

Figure 11: Step-Index MMF

In other words, the refractive index of the core of the step index fiber is constant throughout the core.

Multimode step-index fibers have relatively large core diameters and large numerical apertures. A large core size and a large numerical aperture make it easier to couple light from a Light-Emitting Diode (LED) into the fiber.

Rays of light enter the fiber with different angles to the fiber axis. Rays that enter with a shallower angle travel by a more direct path, and arrive sooner than those which enter at steeper angles. The arrival of different modes of the light at different times is called **Modal Dispersion**.

These alternate paths cause the different groups of light rays, referred to as modes, to arrive separately at the receiving point. The pulse, an aggregate of different modes, begins to spread out, losing its well-defined shape. The need to leave spacing between pulses to prevent overlapping limits the amount of information that can be sent. This type of fiber is best suited for transmission over short distances.

This modal dispersion puts a limit on step-index multimode fibers' bandwidth.

The step-index profile is used in SMFs as well as in MMFs and is characterized by low attenuation and high bandwidth properties for small distances.

Multimode Fibers Types

The types of MMFs are referred to using the term "Optical Multimode" or OM, following the ISO/IEC 11801 designation.

MMFs implementations are characterized by their low cost compared to SMFs. They use 850 nm wavelength LED and Vertical-Cavity Surface-Emitting Lasers (VCSELs).

They can support Ethernet standards ranging from 10 Mbps to 100 Gbps speeds.

There are four types of OMs as depicted in Table 1:

OM	Core/Cladding	IEEE Ethernet Standard Support
OM1	62.5/125	10Base-T
OM2	50/125	100Base-T
OM3	50/125	1GBase-T and 10GBase-T
OM4	50/125	40GBase-T and 100GBase-T

Table 1: MMFs Types

OM1

It is found in legacy cabling systems built from the mid 80s till the 90s. It uses the 62.5/125 µm (core/cladding) MMF and was the FDDI fiber de-facto standard during that period.

There was a good coupling between the 62.5 µm fiber's core and the 850 nm wavelength' LEDs and which could support a distance of 2 kilometers at 10 Mbps.

OM2

This 50 µm fiber's core was used for long haul and short-reach applications in the 70s. However, with the introduction of the SMF in the 80s for long haul telephony applications, 50 µm fibers were left for short-reach interconnects spreading distances ranging from 300 meters to 2000 meters.

In 1995, the 50/100 (core/cladding) MMF was re-established and used as the best solution for the IEEE 100Base-T Ethernet standard because of the lower fiber attenuation that occur at 1300 nm wavelength but for LAN applications only.

Because the 850 nm wavelength LEDs used with the 50 µm core had a bad coupling and provided support for limited distances, the solution consisted to use LEDs at 1300 nm wavelength to compensate for the coupling loss to support the same 2 kilometers as in OM1 but at 100 Mbps.

OM3

This type of Laser Optimized MMF was introduced in 1999. The IEEE Gigabit Ethernet standard published in 1998 specified low cost 850 nm wavelength VCSELs that can reach 1000 meters at Gigabit speed over 50 µm fiber.

In comparison, 62.5 µm fiber or OM1 allows only a distance between 220 and 275 for the same speed.

It also supports 10 Gbps Ethernet standard published in 2002 over runs of 300 meters using 850 nm VCSELs. In contrast, OM1 would only support a distance run between 26 and 33 meters for the same speed.

OM4

It is available in the market since 2005 and is backward compatible with OM3. OM4 uses 850 nm wavelength VCSELs for connecting buildings, backbones and campuses. It supports 10 Gbps Ethernet speed over 550 meters and 40 to 100 Gbps Ethernet applications up to 150 meters.
To achieve the 40 to 100 Gbps, OM4 uses parallel VCSEL Arrays with parallel transmission paths. This is not the case with the 10 Gbps speed where a single serial VCSEL is used, and this is the case with OM3 and for the same speed as well.

Table 2 summaries the properties of all OM types seen above:

OM Type	Jacket Color	Core Diameter (μm)	1 Gbps	10 Gbps	100 Gbps
OM1	Orange	62.5	300 m	33 m	NA
OM2	Orange	50	750 m	82 m	NA
OM3	Aqua	50 (Laser-Optimized)	1000 m	300 m	100 m
OM4	Aqua	50 (Laser-Optimized)	1100 m	550 m	150 m

Table 2: OM Types for Gigabit Speeds using 850 nm Wavelength

Starting from 2008, more 50 μm MMFs are sold compared to 62.5 μm MMFs while OM3/OM4 has been a majority of 50 μm since 2007 according to the "Burroughs Report".
TIA and IEC recommend the use of laser-optimized 50 μm MMF for backbone cabling, single buildings, or corporate campuses for cost effectiveness. It supports higher speeds over relatively long distances compared to LEDs with 62.5 μm core MMF.

While OM1 and OM2 work well with LEDs, OM3 and OM4 fibers can support even longer distances but transceiver specification change is required.

Fiber Optics Wavelengths

There are three prime wavelengths used in fiber optics inside LANs; 850 nm, 1300 nm, and 1500 nm. While MMFs are designated to operate at 850 and 1300 nm LEDs wavelengths, SMFs are optimized for 1310 and 1500 nm using Lasers. With a 1310 nm laser wavelength, SMFs can reach distances between 50 and 100 kilometers, whereas with a 1500 nm laser wavelength, longer distances are supported.
For slower LANs, MMFs rely on the 850 and 1300 nm LEDs wavelengths to support speeds of 10 Mbps and 100 Mbps, while or faster LANs running at 10, 40 and 100 Gbps, MMFs are used with 850 and 1300 nm VCSELs wavelengths.
Recent telecom systems use wavelength-division multiplexing (WDM). In these systems, lasers are chosen with precise wavelengths closely spaced - but not so close they interfere with each other - and transmitted simultaneously on a single fiber. WDM can use the full range of wavelengths between 1260 and 1670 nm in various bands.

The WDM technique allows full duplex communication on a single fiber strand using different laser wavelengths.

Bend-Insensitive Multimode Fiber – BIMMF

BIMMF has an innovative core design that enables it to significantly reduce macro bend loss even in the most challenging bend scenarios, Figure 12.

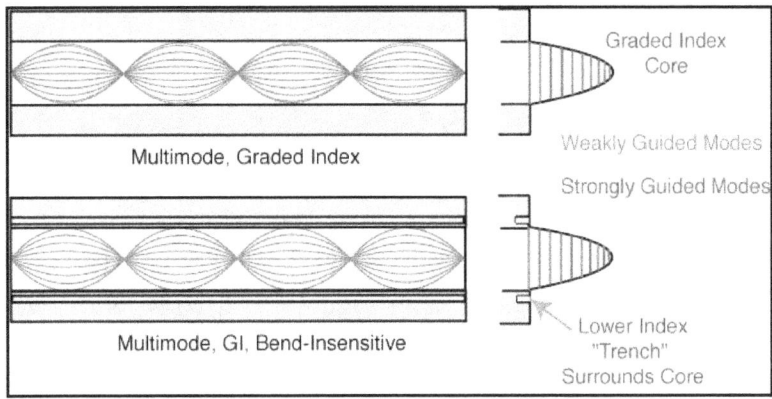

Figure 12: MMF Graded Index versus BIMMF

Optical fiber manufacturers use a refractive index or *trench*, which is a ring of lower refractive index material surrounding the core of the fiber to reflect the lost light back into the core.
BIMMF is fully compliant with the OM2, OM3 and OM4 standards for laser-optimized fibers and is also backward compatible with the installed base of 50-μm multimode fibers.
BIMMF was first introduced as a way to improve cable management in large data centers. Discussions about BIMMF in standards groups began in April 2010.
Many BIMMFs being installed today may have bandwidth and connection losses that vary significantly from the standard MMFs in the embedded base.
By 2014 all major fiber manufacturers had switched to BIMMFs as their standard offering.

Higher Speed Fiber Links using MMFs

To increase the speed over MMFs in data centers, parallel-optics technology is preferred for transmission over relatively short distances with less than 300 meters.
This technique consists of running multiple fibers simultaneously in parallel to provide the required speed, Figure 13.

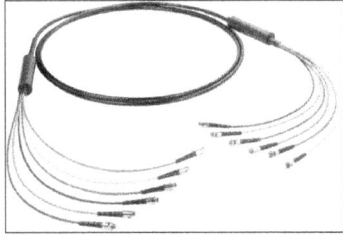

Figure 13: Multiple Fibers Running in Parallel

These multiple fibers are packaged as one cable, as depicted in Figure 14 with one connector at each end of the cable.

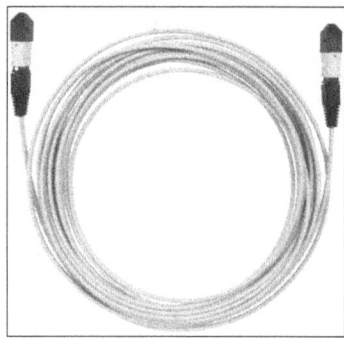

Figure 14: Multiple Fibers Trunk Cable

Another example shows a fan-out cable as in Figure 15. It consists of twelve MMFs connectors at one end and one connector at the other end.

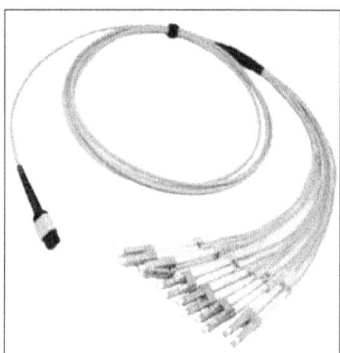

Figure 15: Multiple Fibers Fan-Out Cables

A multi-fiber connector is required to connect these MMFs, Figure 16. This connector is known as Multi-fiber Push On – MPO connector. Sometimes, another term is used; MTP which stands for Mechanical Transfer Push On. MTP is nothing but a registered trademark of "US Conec" and identifies a specific brand of the MPO style connector.

Figure 16: MPO/MTP connector

The MTP product complies with the MPO standard. Therefore, the MTP connector is an MPO connector. In the remaining part of this section, we will use the term MPO to refer to the multiple-fiber connector.

MPO connectors have either a 12-fiber or 24-fiber array to support a high speed solution, Figure 17.

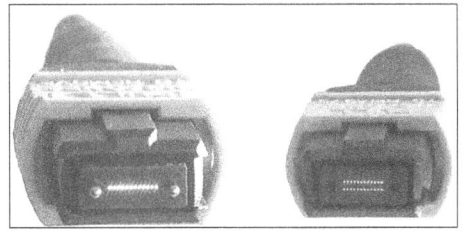

Figure 17: 12-Fiber (Left) and 24-Fiber (Right) MPO connectors

Although, multiple-fiber trunk and fan-out cables are used with OM1 and OM2 MMFs, however for 10, 40 and 100 Gbps speeds, OM3/OM4 MMFs should be used.
These multiple MMFs are aggregated to form the channels that provide the required speeds. For example to build a 40 Gbps link over fiber using a single wavelength, four 10-Gbps fibers are deployed for transmit and another four 10-Gbps fiber are deployed for receive, Figure 18.

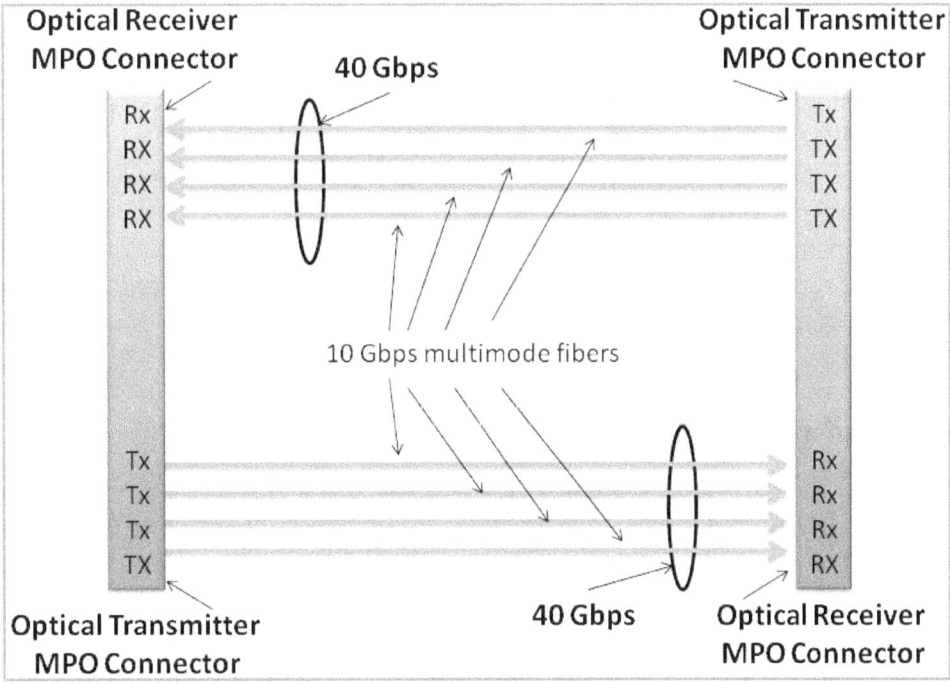

Figure 18: 40-Gbps Parallel Optics Transmission

With the 40-Gbps high speed solution, 8 of the 12 fibers are up and used for transmission. The same is done to reach a 100 Gbps over fiber where ten 10-Gbps fibers are brought together for transmit and another set of ten 10-Gbps fibers are deployed for receive, Figure 19.

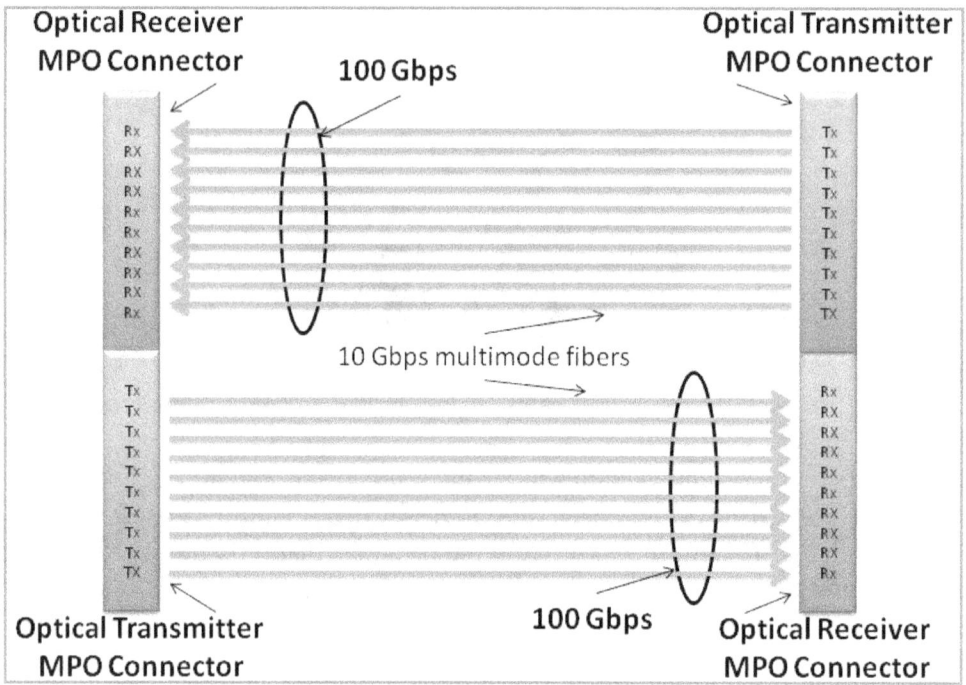

Figure 19: 100-Gbps Parallel Optics Transmission

The 100 Gbps using a single wavelength can be achieved with 2 x 12 fiber MPO connectors or 1 x 24 fiber MPO connector configuration.
Although both options can be utilized, a 2 x 12 fiber MPO connector provides better insertion and return loss performance.
With the 100-Gbps high speed solution, 20 of the 24 fibers are up and used for transmission. Parallel optics is often the most cost effective solution for getting 40 and 100 Gigabit per second transmission of data over distances exceeding 100 meters but less than 300 meters and using MMFs.

Comparison of Light Sources

Both lasers and LEDs are used as light sources. Laser light sources are significantly more expensive than LED light sources however they produce a light that can be precisely controlled and which has a high power. Because the LED light sources produce a more dispersed light source (many modes of light) these light sources are used with multi-mode cable. With a laser source which produces close to a single mode of light, single-mode fibers are used. However, for a better coupling between the light and the fiber core of a MMF, a laser light can also be used as this is the case with OM3 and OM4.
It should be noted that the length of a fiber optic cable run is primarily determined by the strength of the light source.

Fiber Optic connectors

Optical fibers are connected to terminal equipment by optical fiber connectors. These connectors are usually of a standard type such as FC, SC, ST, LC, and MTRJ
An optical fiber connector terminates the end of an optical fiber, and enables quicker connection and disconnection.

While there are many different types of fiber connectors, they share similar design characteristics. Simplex vs. duplex: Simplex means 1 connector per end while duplex means 2 connectors per end, Figure 20.

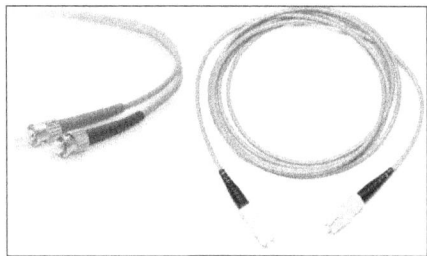

Figure 20: Duplex (left) versus Simplex (right) Fiber Optic Cable

FC Connector

FC stands for Fixed Connection, Figure 21. FC connectors are typical in test environments and for single mode applications. They were designed for use in high-vibration environments and come in simplex configuration only.

FC connector has a screw-on mechanism and supports both single mode as well as multimode.

It was the most popular single mode connector for many years. However, it has been gradually replaced by SC and LC connectors.

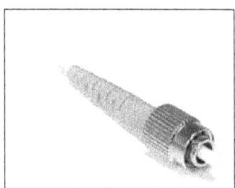

Figure 21: FC Connector

ST Connector

The ST connector was one of the first connector types widely implemented in fiber optic networking applications, Figure 22. Originally developed by AT&T, it stands for Straight Tip connector.

ST is a Common connector for multimode fibers. Although extremely popular for many years (late 80s and early 90s), the ST connector has been supplanted by smaller, denser connectors in many installations.

Figure 22: ST Connector

SC Connector

SC stands for Subscriber Connector (Square Connector or Standard Connector) a general purpose push/pull style Connector developed by NTT (the Japanese telecommunications company). The SC connector is available in both Simplex (Figure 23) and Duplex configurations (Figure 24) and is used with Single mode as well as Multimode optic fiber. It offers low cost, simplicity, and durability.

Figure 23: Simplex SC Connector

Figure 24: Duplex SC Connector

MIC Connector

The SC connector was closely related to MIC connector (Figure 25) which housed two SC connectors in a single shell and was used for FDDI networks, obsolete by now.

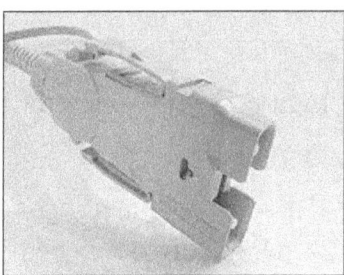

Figure 25: MIC Connector

Modern Fiber Optic connectors

LC connector

LC stands for Lucent Connector. The LC is a small form-factor fiber optic connector. It comes in simplex (Figure 26) and duplex (Figure 27) configurations and supports both single mode and multimode.
The LC has good performance and is highly favored for single mode.

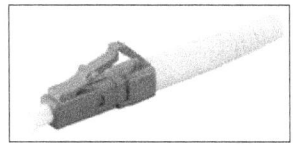

Figure 26: Simplex LC Connector

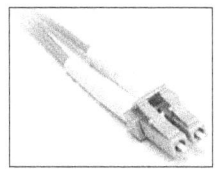

Figure 27: Duplex LC Connector MT-RJ (connector)

MT-RJ stands for Mechanical Transfer Registered Jack. It comes in duplex configuration only and supports multimode fiber optic only, Figure 28.

Figure 28: MT-RJ Connector

The MT-RJ is one of the newly emerging small form factor connectors that are becoming more common in the networking industry. The MT-RJ utilizes two fibers and integrates them into a single design.
It is half the size of the SC connector it was designed to replace. Compared to single-fiber terminations such as SC, the MT-RJ Connector offers lower Termination cost and greater density for both electronics and cable management hardware.

Degrading Properties

A certain number of factors contribute in degrading the light pulse signal in a fiber optic cable:

Attenuation

It results from the glass fiber absorbing the energy of the light, Figure 29. The rate at which it is absorbed depends on the wavelength of the light and the characteristics of the particular glass.
Attenuation of a given wavelength of light is measured in decibel per kilometer (db/km).
There is a maximum amount of degradation that can be tolerated before the link fails to operate properly.

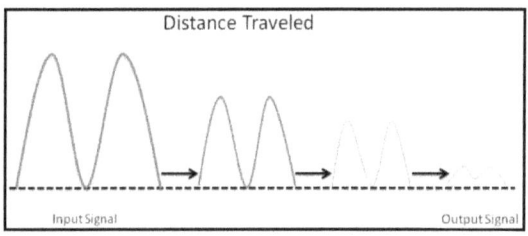

Figure 29: Attenuation

Dispersion

It is the effect of spreading out that occurs as the light travels down the cable. A short pulse of light gradually becomes longer and eventually falls back far enough that the next pulse overlaps with it, Figure 30.

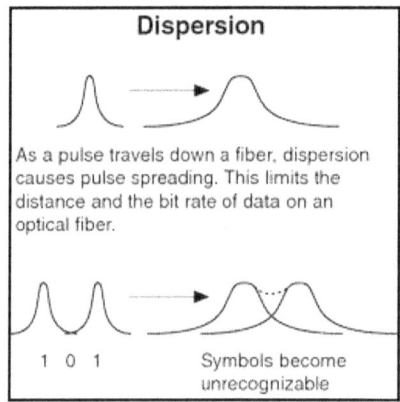

Figure 30: Dispersion

Latest Developments in Single Mode Optical Fibers

Currently, the fastest commercial single-laser-single-fiber is for Ethernet network connection and that can send information at a speed of 100 Gbps.

The IEEE is investigating the feasibility of either a 400 Gbps or 1 Tbps Ethernet standard with ratification not done until 2017 or later.

For long haul connections using optical fibers, many attempts to boost the speed have seen light from research work in different Universities.

In 2009, the Denmark Technical University (DTU) was the first to break the 1-Tbps barrier using many-cored fibers and dozens of lasers.

In 2011, researchers at Germany's Karlsruhe Institute of technology achieved 26 Tbps using a single-laser-single optical-fiber.

In July 2014, the DTU announced it has reached 43 Tbps using a single-laser over a multi-cored fiber (7 cores) produced by the Japanese Telecom NTT.

In October 2014, researchers from the University of Florida and Eindhoven University of technology developed a new fiber optic medium that allows data to be sent and received at up to 255 Tbps. They used 7 fibers in a multi-core configuration where each fiber has less than 200 μm of diameter.

It should be noted that these many-cored solutions are too complex for general commercial use. However, there is a high optimism in developing even faster speeds using a single laser on a single optical fiber.

More recently, photonics researchers at the University of California, San Diego, increased the maximum power at which optical signals can be sent through optical fibers by almost 20 times the base level. This was published in the June 26 2015 issue of the journal Science.

In lab experiment, information was sent 12000 kilometers through fiber optic cables with standard amplifiers and no repeaters.

Summary about Fiber Optic Cables

In the current state of technology, the copper cables have gained in performance and are able to provide cabling solutions to support higher speeds such as 10, 40 and 100 Gbps.

The fiber optic cables are no more considered as the best choice when it comes to high speed data transfer.

Advantages of Fiber over Copper Cables

Fiber optic cables offer a number of advantages over copper cables. These advantages are listed below:

1. The number of fiber cables that can be connected on a patch panel is larger than with the copper cables; fiber cables have a higher density in terms of cables size and connector's size.
2. The power consumption of fiber is around 0.5 W and is much smaller compared to copper cables power consumption.
3. Testing of a fiber optic cable installation is quicker and faster compared to copper cables.
4. Fiber optic cables can run longer distances than copper. The distance can range from hundreds of meters to tens of kilometers without the need of a repeater depending on fiber material.
5. Optical Fiber Cables do not have speed limits or bandwidth limitations. They can support any speed/ bandwidth depending only on the type of active components used at either end.
6. It is enough to replace the active components at either end of a link in order to upgrade the fiber communication to support higher bandwidths. There is no need to change all the underlying cabling.
7. Since the data moving is made of light, it does not radiate electromagnetic signals which make it difficult to tap with an external device.
8. The fiber optic conductor is a core made of glass or pure plastic with no conductivity for electrical current. Therefore, fiber optic cables do not have problems caused by EMI and crosstalk as in copper conductors. In optical fibers, the crosstalk problem does exist but is different from its counterpart in copper conductors. It occurs between different wavelengths carrying information in a single optical fiber in full duplex mode. It also occurs between neighboring fibers to alter the absorption spectrum of the fibers.
9. In fact, many problems faced by copper cables are simply non-existent in fiber cables.

10. The proliferation and lower costs of media converters are making copper to fiber migration much easier.
11. Advancements in technology have made terminating and using fiber easier.
12. The cost for fiber cable, components, and hardware has steadily decreased. Overall, fiber cable is more expensive than copper cable in the short run, but it may be less expensive in the long run since they last longer than copper cables.
13. Fiber typically costs less to maintain, has less downtime, and requires less networking hardware. In addition, advances in field termination technology have reduced the cost of fiber installation as well. Low cost 850 nm wavelength laser could challenge copper PHY cost.
14. Because no electricity is passed through optical fibers, there is no fire hazard.
15. An optical cable weighs less than a comparable copper wire cable. Optical fibers can be drawn to smaller diameters than copper wire.

Disadvantages of Fiber Optic Cables

The fiber optic cables have some disadvantages, as well:

1. The optical transceivers are more expensive compared to those of copper cables.
2. Even though the raw material for making optical fibers; sand, is abundant and cheap, optical fibers are still more expensive per meter than copper.
3. Optical fibers are more fragile than copper wires.
4. The glass, used to manufacture a fiber, can be affected by various chemicals.
5. Building an optical fiber cable is not an easy process like this is the case with the copper cable. Usually, it requires extensive training with expensive equipment and tools.
6. Fibers can be broken or have transmission loses when wrapped around curves of only a few centimeters radius.
7. Optical fibers require more protection around the cable compared to copper.

www.ingramcontent.com/pod-product-compliance
Lightning Source LLC
Chambersburg PA
CBHW080945170526
45158CB00008B/2382